ARBITRATION IN ENGLAND AND GERMANY

BY

DR. RUDOLF KAHN

BARRISTER-AT-LAW; ADVOCATE AT THE HIGH COURTS AT BERLIN

(Reprinted from the "Journal of Comparative Legislation," Vol. XII, 1930)

LONDON:
SOCIETY OF COMPARATIVE LEGISLATION,
1 ELM COURT, TEMPLE, E.C.4.
1930.

In Kommission bei
J. Schweitzer Verlag (Arthur Sellier)
München, Berlin und Leipzig

Printed in Great Britain by Hazell, Watson & Viney, Ltd.,
London and Aylesbury.

CONTENTS

ARBITRATION IN ENGLAND AND GERMANY,

A STUDY IN COMPARATIVE LEGISLATION AND CONFLICT OF LAWS.

[*Contributed by* DR. RUDOLF KAHN.]

Definition of Arbitration.—For the purpose of this inquiry "Arbitration" may be defined as the proceedings and determination of a dispute by a tribunal other than the ordinary courts of a country and competent to decide by agreement of the parties.

The general principles relating to arbitration are contained for England in the Arbitration Act, 1889 (52 & 53 Vict., c. 49) hereinafter called the Arbitration Act, and the Administration of Justice Act, 1920 (10 & 11 Geo. V, c. 81); for Germany in the tenth book of the *Zivilprozessordnung* of January 30, 1877 (hereinafter abbreviated *Z.P.O.*) as amended by later statutes.

For England the statutory provisions of the Arbitration Act are supplemented by the Common Law. The principles governing arbitration proceedings in both countries are either such as must apply or may be applied, or are to be applied by implication of law, if there is no provision to the contrary.

Outside our inquiry remain references to arbitration under special statutes [1] or by order of the court in default of consent,[2] in England, or reference by consent to an ordinary court as arbitrator [3] in Germany.

What Matters may be referred.—The Arbitration Act does not define what matters may be brought to arbitration, but the proposition seems to be that all disputes are referable to arbitration with the exception of cases where criminal matters or proceedings are involved, of a nature which the policy of English law would not permit to be compromised, or where charges of fraud are involved, or where the matter to be decided is contaminated by illegality.[4]

[1] For England there are numerous special statutes, as *e.g.* Companies Clauses Act, 1845 (8 & 9 Vict., c. 16), Public Health Act, 1875 (38 & 39 Vict., c. 55), etc. For Germany Gerverbegerichtsgesetz, v. 29, Juli 1890; Gesetz betr. Kaufmannsgerichte, vol. 6, Juli 1904.

[2] Ss. 13, 14, Arbitration Act.

[3] Beschleunigungs Verordnung, v. 22, XII, 1923; see also Friedrich Stein, *Die Zivilprozessordnung für das Deutsche Reich*, 13th ed., vol. i, p. 1155.

[4] See Russell on *Arbitration and Awards*, 11th ed., p. 1, ss.; Roger T. Bacon, *Commercial Arbitration*, p. 22, ss.; Earl of Halsbury, *The Laws of England*, 1907, vol. i, p. 444.

By 1025 of the German *Z.P.O.* all matters of dispute as to legal rights may be referred to arbitration, provided that such disputes would, in default of arbitration, have been tried by the ordinary German civil courts [1] and the parties would have been entitled to compromise their subject-matter of dispute.

The distinction [2] between the subject-matters referable to arbitration under English and German law may be summarized as follows:

In the first instance, under German law no criminal matters, *even such as could legally form the subject of a compromise*, are referable to arbitration; but, on the other hand, actions in tort involving fraud may be tried by arbitration. It is further apparent that, the notions of crime and tort in both countries being different, they produce different effects in the subject-matter of arbitration. *E.g.* an indictment for non-repair of a highway cannot be referred to arbitration under English law,[3] because it is a criminal matter of a non-compromisable character, whereas in Germany it may be in case of non-feasance a matter purely for the administrative courts, and for this reason not be referable to arbitration.

On the other side the law relating to libel and slander, which forms an important part of the English Law of Torts, is under German law mainly of a criminal nature, and therefore not referable to arbitration. An award to the effect that one party shall beg the other's pardon would be impossible under German law because of its criminal nature.[4]

As to matters contaminated with illegality, I think the proposition is identical in both countries, subject to the differences in the conception of "illegality." This question touches also the validity and effects of a submission.

There is, however, one great distinction between the two systems of law as to what may form the subject-matter of an arbitration and this distinction is not very apparent on the face of the above definitions.

In German Law Reference must be of whole Matter in Dispute.—Under German law only such matters may be referred to arbitration as would otherwise form the subject-matter of a trial by a civil court.[5]

This means that the whole subject-matter of dispute must be submitted to the court for the purpose of a *condemnatio* defining the legal relationship of the parties. Mere elements of a subject-matter in dispute cannot

[1] This restriction, although not apparent on the face of 1025, *Z.P.O.*, is clearly established; see Stein, *Vorbem.*, II. 2 to 1025, vol. ii, p. 1024.

[2] Reference will be made sometimes to an article in *The Law Quarterly Review*, vol. xliii, p. 205, by Mr. E. C. Weiss on "Arbitration in Germany." I am unable to agree with Mr. Weiss on many important points. Professor A. Nussbaum, Berlin Editor of the *Internationales Jahrbuch für Schiedsgerichtswesen* (Berlin, Carl Heymanns, Verlag) dealt with some of Mr. Weiss's statements in vol. ii, p. 384, of his Yearbook.

[3] *R.* v. *Blakemore* [1850] 14 Q.B. 544.

[4] *Glover* v. *Barrie* [1699] 1 Salk 71.

[5] *Entscheidungen des Reichsgerichts in Zivilsachen* (in the following abbreviated *R.G.*), vol. 67, p. 73.

be submitted to the decision of the German courts, and can, therefore, not form the subject-matter of an arbitration in the technical meaning. This may best be illustrated by a case decided by the Reichsgericht.[1]

In the dissolution of a partnership, one partner was to take over the share of the other. In the course of the dispute as to the sums payable by the purchasing partner to the other, both partners agreed that an arbitrator should decide the value of the property belonging to the partnership. It was held that what purported to be an arbitration was not an arbitration in spite of what the partners may have termed it, because the subject-matter of the dispute was the purchase price of the share of the partner, and no German court could have entertained an action merely for the valuation of the partnership's property, seeing that this was only an element of the matter in dispute, namely the definition of the compensation payable to the other partner, and the arbitrator stands in the shoes of an ordinary court.

Declaratory Quasi-arbitrations.—This decision leads also to some remarks in respect of declaratory judgments under § 256, *Z.P.O.* The rule is, that no declaratory judgment may be sought unless the plaintiff can prove a legal interest in an early declaratory judgment, *i.e.* in other words that though he cannot yet ask the court for a judgment ordering the defendant to do some act, he has, nevertheless, a legal interest in an early declaratory rule for the future.

The position is here much the same as it was in England before October 1883, when it was provided by order XXV, r. 5, that the court was free to make binding declarations of right.[2] It follows, therefore, that an arbitrator cannot make an award of a declaratory nature, if the court could not have done so. But as long as there is a *prima facie* legal interest of the plaintiff in the early declaratory determination of his rights, an award may not be impeached for this reason, because the discretion as to the legal interest vests in the arbitrator as it would otherwise have vested in the court.[3] Such quasi-arbitrations—in German called *Schiedsgutachten*—follow the rules of arts. 317 ss. of the German Civil Code.[4]

Determination of Contractual Obligation.—As distinct from these cases which, for the above reason, cannot be arbitrations in the technical sense of German law, are to be mentioned the cases where either a third named person has to determine an obligation left undefined by the contract (s. 317, German Civil Code), or a third person has to declare with binding effect the as yet undefined contractual obligation of a party, which obligation, however, is definable by the provisions of the contract itself.[5] In the first case the third person may either have absolute discretion or only a judicial discretion. The first case is clearly not

[1] *Entscheidungen des Reichsgerichts in Zivilsachen* (in the following abbreviated *R.G.*), vol. 67, p. 73.

[2] W. Blake Odgers, *Principles of Procedure*, 5th ed., p. 205.

[3] *R.G.*, vol. 100, p. 121. [4] *Ibid.*, vol. 96, p. 60. [5] *Ibid.*

arbitration, and follows also the rules of arts. 317 ss. German Civil Code, but it seems that the latter case may under certain conditions form the subject-matter of an arbitration according to the intention of the parties. The conditions would be that the determination of the contractual obligation constitutes the whole subject-matter in dispute, and that there is some legal interest in an early declaratory award.

Under English law a similar problem arises, although an arbitrator would certainly be free to decide an element[1] being a component part of a subject-matter in dispute.

Distinction between Valuer and Arbitrator.—The problem here deals with valuations, and the problem is not less difficult than under German law. Here again we find that, as Neville J. puts it,[2] " you cannot make a valuer an arbitrator by calling him so, or *vice versa*."

Instances of agreements where parties agree to sell goods at a price fixed by a third person do not constitute real arbitrations under English law,[3] although they may lead to proper arbitration if, after a dispute as to the price having arisen, the dispute is referred for arbitration to a third person. Again, if a third person is intended only to use his own judgment and skill as a valuer without holding an inquiry in the nature of a judicial inquiry, he is only a valuer and not an arbitrator.[4] These are the general principles, but cases of an intermediate kind may present great difficulties. In view of *Chambers* v. *Goldthorpe* [1901] 1 Q.B. 624,[5] where no actual dispute had arisen before the award, I think there is a good ground for the submission that under English law, as under German law, no arbitration arises where a third party has to fix an obligation left undefined by the contract; but arbitration may arise where this third party has merely to declare the obligation arising under a contract and define it according to the intrinsic contents of the contract, and the proceeding is in the nature of a judicial inquiry, irrespective of whether the third person is to use his expert skill and knowledge or not.

Who may refer Matters to Arbitration.—(*a*) *English Law.*—" Every person who has a right of which he can dispose is competent to submit questions affecting that right to arbitration "[6] under English law. It may be of interest to consider shortly various classes of persons, where the right of disposal or capacity of acting may be questionable.

Married women are, since the Married Women's Property Acts, 1882 (45 & 46 Vict., c. 75) and 1893 (56 & 57 Vict., c. 63), as freely able to submit to arbitration as a *feme sole*.[7]

By common law an infant cannot submit to arbitration, except in

[1] Bacon, *op. cit.*, p. 22.
[2] *Taylor* v. *Yielding*, 1912, 56; *Solic. Journal*, p. 253.
[3] Russell, *op. cit.*, p. 329.
[4] *In re Hammond and Waterton* [1890] 62 L.T. 808.
[5] See also *Tharsis Sulphur Co.* v. *Loftus*, 4. C.P.D., p. 148.
[6] Russell, *op. cit.*, p. 18.
[7] The rules relating to " restraint from anticipation " are mainly preserved by s. 1 of the Married Women's Property Act, 1893.

the case of reasonable contracts for necessaries or service or contracts plainly for the benefit of the infant himself, and by the Infant's Relief Act, 1874 (37 & 38 Vict., c. 62), a ratification of a contract by the infant after attaining full age is equally voidable by the infant.

A bankrupt can submit to arbitration, but without affecting the creditors' rights. The trustees in bankruptcy may refer a particular case to arbitration with the permission of the committee of inspection.

A partner, although an agent of the firm, and his other partners for the purpose of the business of the partnership,[1] cannot bind the firm or his partners by a submission, because entering into a submission is no part of the ordinary business of a trading firm.[2] Actual authority or subsequent ratification, whether implied or expressed, is, however, sufficient.

Agents may submit on behalf of their principals to arbitration, if authorized to do so. The general common law rules as to agency are applicable. It seems that an agent can refer to arbitration in writing, although his own authority was only oral.[3] But to enter into a submission by deed, his authority must also be by deed.[4]

A solicitor has no implied authority to refer to arbitration before the action, but where an action is already proceeding such authority may be implied in respect of the subject-matter of the action.[5]

Counsel has full power to submit to arbitration matters properly belonging to the case,[6] but the court may set aside the reference, if counsel has acted against express instructions of his client even unknown to the other party.[7]

(*b*) *German Law.*—Under German law the general principles of the law of contract equally apply when determining the right and capacity to refer to arbitration. It may be worth while to contrast the principles laid down for the English law. The German law requires both capacity to act in law and the right of disposal.[8]

Infants under seven years and lunatics so found by inquisition are incapable of acting; the submissions of minors from seven to twenty-one years are void without the consent of their legal representatives, because a submission can never be merely beneficial within the meaning of § 107, B.G.B.[9] Women, either married or unmarried, are fully capable of acting in law, but married women cannot, as a rule, submit to arbitration without concurrence of their husbands, because under the Statutory Regime, § 1363, B.G.B., and most of the contractual regimes, the wife has not the right or sole right of disposal. A bankrupt can refer to arbitration, but without affecting the rights of the creditors (§ 7, *Konkursordnung* of February 10, 1877, with later amend-

[1] S. 5, Partnership Act, 1890 (53 & 54 Vict., c. 39).
[2] *Stead* v. *Salt* [1825] 3 Bing, p. 103.
[3] Russell, *op. cit.*, p. 28; Bacon, *op. cit.*, p. 27.
[4] *Ibid.*, p. 29.
[5] *Ibid.*; Bacon, *op. cit.*, p. 28.
[6] *Matthews* v. *Munster* [1887] 20 Q.B.D. 141.
[7] Russell, *op. cit.*, p. 554.
[8] Stein, *op. cit.*, vol. ii, p. 1030.
[9] B.G.B. = German Civil Code.

ments), otherwise the receiver in bankruptcy, with the consent of the committee of inspection, is solely entitled to refer (§ 133, s. 2, § 136, *Konkursordnung*).

In regard to agency the following broad principles may be mentioned. An authorized agent may refer to arbitration, a submission by an unauthorized agent requires ratification by the principal (§ 177, B.G.B.). In default of ratification the agent remains liable (§ 179, B.G.B.) There in an important right of the other party to the submission to call upon the alleged principal to declare his intention of ratification within two weeks of the date of the communication of the request, and any subsequent ratification is inoperative unless communicated within two weeks (§ 177, B.G.B.). It must also be noted that the German law does not recognize undisclosed agency. The power of an agent to refer may clearly be conferred orally and does not require any form (§ 1672, B.G.B.).

In the case of mercantile employees it is necessary to distinguish between *Procura* and other mercantile powers of agency. The holder of a *Procura* can refer (§ 49, H.G.B.),[1] whereas an ordinary mercantile agent cannot refer without express authority (§ 54, H.G.B.). A partner can under German law validly refer to arbitration as against the firm or other partners, and irrespective of his being properly authorized or not (§ 126, H.G.B.[2]) A German advocate is not by his retainer authorized to refer. This rule holds good, whether litigation has already been started or not.

Who may be Arbitrator.—(*a*) *English Law.*—Under English law it seems that the parties may appoint persons of any mental or physical imperfection, or even infants or lunatics, provided the parties knew the disability, or ought to have known it, when making the appointment.[3]

"The underlying principle is, that the parties choose their arbitrators for some good reason, and if they know or ought to have known, that they were not impartial in the ordinary sense of the word, it is no duty of the court to interfere."[4]

The following qualifications arise from the above general statement.

Disabilities in the person of an arbitrator will not affect an appointment if both parties know it or ought to have known it before the appointment, disabilities arising subsequent to the appointment, but before the opening of the hearing, may invalidate the appointment, provided the parties object either at the opening, if they knew the disabilities then, or at some later date.[5] There is no strict rule as to what interest or personal misconduct of the arbitrator is a disability, the principle being that in order to upset an appointment it must be "inequitable that the parties should be held bound by the agreement

[1] Handelsgesetzbuch of May 10, 1897, with later amendments.

[2] See Mittelstein in Nussbaum's *Yearbook*, vol. i, p. 39.

[3] Viner's *Abridgement*, "Arbitrement," A2, vol. iii, p. 41; Russell, *op. cit.*, p. 34; Bacon, *op. cit.*, p. 18.

[4] *Per* Lord Justice Bowen in *Jackson* v. *Barry Rly. Co.* [1893] 1 Ch., p. 247.

[5] Russell, *op. cit.*, p. 43.

to accept his decision."[1] It is also noteworthy that an arbitrator may be a witness in the case submitted to arbitration,[2] but this seems only possible if an umpire has been appointed.

It seems also to be recognized recently that where a reference is to arbitrators and an umpire, the arbitrators are allowed to act as advocates for the parties,[3] which tends to prove that each party may choose an arbitrator holding a similar view to his.

(*b*) *German Law.*—Under German law the same great latitude of choice of arbitrators is given as under English law. The only limits are that a party, or his representative in law, as *e.g.* a director of a company, cannot be an arbitrator,[4] though an agent may be one, and likewise a person not capable at all to act in law is excluded. But, corresponding to the position in English law, an appointment may be invalidated by either of the parties for the particular disabilities of being under age, deafness, dumbness,[5] or conviction of crime under special circumstances, or for undue delay caused by an arbitrator not named in the submission, and finally for the same reasons, and under the same conditions, as would entitle the party to object to a judge.[6] These reasons and conditions are defined by §§ 41–3, *Z.P.O.* But in the case of a judge the grounds enumerated in § 41, *Z.P.O.*, as *e.g.* relationship, marriage (also dissolved marriage) or previous committal to a certain view in the same cause render a judge unfit in law to act as judge in the same cause, and may, even after judgment, cause the judgment to be set aside (§ 579, s. 2, *Z.P.O.*); on the other hand, the reasons in § 42, *Z.P.O.*, which are, in the main, want of impartiality, entitle a party only to a challenge or objection, and this must have been made as soon as the party learns of the reason for the alleged want of impartiality; after judgment such objection cannot be taken at all, unless an objection taken during the proceedings was refused (§ 579, r. 3, *Z.P.O.*). But, on the other hand, in the case of an arbitrator these grounds of legal incapacity and objection stand on the same footing (§ 42, *Z.P.O.*),[7] so that it is clear that no ground for objection (including those grounds which would incapacitate a judge) can be taken into consideration after the award.[8] As to the time when grounds for

[1] Russell, *op. cit.*, p. 39.

[2] In *Bourgeois* v. *Weddell & Co.* [1924] 1 K.B., p. 539.

[3] See note 2, *supra*, and *French Government* v. *Owners of s.s. "Tsurushima Maru"* [1921] 37 T.L.R. 961.

[4] Stein, *op. cit.*, vol. ii, p. 1028. Under English law it seems a party may act as arbitrator (*Matthew* v. *Ollerton* [1694] Comb. 218; also *R.G.*, vol. 93, p. 288).

[5] The defects of deafness and dumbness may equally incapacitate under English law (Russell, *op. cit.*, p. 35).

[6] § 1032, *Z.P.O.*

[7] *R.G.*, vol. 44, p. 391.

[8] Stein, *op. cit.*, 1041, *Z.P.O.*, N. 17, 18. Mr. Weiss, in 43 *L.Q.R.*, writes on p. 208: "If a party enters on the reference with a knowledge of any defect in an arbitrator, he is bound by the award, *but an award made with the assistance of an arbitrator who might have been challenged had the parties known of any grounds for so doing, can be set aside.*" This, I submit, is wrong, as shown above. And again, p. 210: "The following case may serve as an illustration of this peculiar position.

objection must have arisen or have come to the knowledge of either of the parties, and when objection must have been made, the position is identical with English law. It is quite clear that members of the legal profession, and also judges, can act as arbitrators, and advocates especially frequently do.[1]

Suppose A was appointed by one of the parties, the award is made and nothing seems to be wrong. The award is enforced after an order has been obtained and then, five years afterwards, the other party discovers that the arbitrator was related to the party that appointed him. An action for setting aside the award may be brought within one month. What becomes of the maxim *Quieta non movere* ?"

[1] Mr. Weiss writes on p. 207: "The German courts have, in particular, *regularly set aside* awards made by practising lawyers, and even, frequently, such made by lawyers in the employ of a trade association. As recently as 1926 the Supreme Court at Leipsic dismissed an action by a judge who sued for his costs incurred as arbitrator in an arbitration. The Supreme Court thought that it was incompatible with the duties of a judge to act as arbitrator in the employ of private parties! Surely a view which is not easily comprehensible to an English lawyer, but which is readily intelligible in the light of certain abuses occasionally found in the arbitration in Germany (see, for the decision, *Juristische Wochenschrift*, 1926, p. 1569)."

This statement is most incorrect. Quite apart from the fact that the courts cannot set aside an award, except for special reasons (see later) I have not found any decision where an award has been set aside because of the concurrence of a lawyer or a judge. Mr. Weiss cannot give any authorities for such a statement. The position of an arbitrator under German law is surely not that of an employee, but, as *R.G.*, vol. 94, p. 212, puts it, that of an independent judge, freer than an ordinary judge, but likewise impartial and unprejudiced. The contractual relationship between arbitrator and parties is of a singular nature and is neither agency nor employment (*R.G.*, vol. 41, p. 251; vol. 59, p. 247; vol. 74, p. 323); but the principles of agency or employment may come in as far as applicable in the question of remuneration of the arbitrators and their liability to make an award. Under English law the position is similar and one infers an implied promise to pay remuneration (*Brown* v. *Llandovery Terra-cotta Co., Ltd.* [1909] 25 T.L.R. 625). In the decision quoted by Mr. Weiss (*J.W.*, 1926, p. 1596), where an executor of a deceased judge claimed for remuneration due for an award, the issue was that the defendants alleged that the judge originally dealing with the matter in his judicial office had caused it to be referred to him as an arbitrator for the sake of remuneration. These serious allegations would have, if proved, rendered the contractual arrangement as to remuneration of the arbitrator illegal and void, as being against public policy. Nevertheless, the award would remain valid. (This shows clearly the distinction in the contractual relationship of parties and arbitrators, as to the arbitration itself and other incidentals.) Now in this very decision the *Reichsgericht* says literally: "In accordance with the view of the Court of Appeal, there is no objection to a judge accepting the position of an arbitrator or umpire in an arbitration for reasonable remuneration, if and as long as the independence of a judge and the administration of justice are not prejudiced. But there must not be created a kind of dependent and paid relationship. As a rule the conditions are satisfied if the arbitration is undertaken only for the single case, and not permanently for the same parties, and if the judge and the parties are at any time free in their acceptance and their choice." As one observes, these and the following remarks deal only with the etiquette of the German bench and would certainly be observed equally by an English judge. They do not touch the validity of an award. Mr. Weiss has here made a grave mistake.

Also administrative bodies may be arbitrators, if this is compatible with their public duties.[1] It is equally possible to refer to a judge (not named) of a certain court, in which case the holder of the office in his capacity as a private individual is referred to.[2]

Effect of the Submission and Revocation of a Submission.—(*a*) *English Law.*—The submission and its effects under English law are the subject of highly developed rules.

I. S. 27 of the Arbitration Act defines " submission " : " Unless the contrary intention appears," it " means a written agreement to submit present or future differences to arbitration, whether an arbitrator is named or not." The definition is somewhat inaccurate, for, *e.g.*, s. 1 of the Act cannot include an agreement to refer future differences, but must necessarily only apply to an agreement to refer existing disputes to a named arbitrator, *i.e.* be a " submission " as it was understood before the Act. These technicalities, although of great importance to English law, are not of interest to our present inquiry, which in addition is only confined to the law at present. As it appears by the definition, the agreement must be in writing, which may be by correspondence or even by incorporation of another document containing the clause. Signature may be necessary by the party to be charged if it comes within the Statute of Frauds or the Sale of Goods Act. A corporation can as a rule only refer under its common seal. A parol submission is nevertheless valid, although it does not come under the Act. But their great disadvantages are the possibility of disputes as to the exact terms used, that they cannot be enforced by attachment [3] and that they can be revoked at any time before the award is made.[4] It is noteworthy in this connexion that a general agreement in writing to refer future disputes to one or more persons to be appointed and a subsequent parol submission in pursuance of the general agreement remains a parol submission and does not come within the Act.[5] Therefore also the submission of a present dispute must be in writing, or at least the appointment of the arbitrators must be so.

S. 1 of the Arbitration Act deals with the revocation of a submission. The terms are : " A submission, unless a contrary intention is expressed therein, shall be irrevocable, except by leave of the court or a judge, and shall have the same effect in all respects as if it had been made an order of court." [6]

[1] Case of a *Provinziallandtag* in *R.G.*, vol. 13, p. 407.

[2] *R.G.*, vol. 53, p. 1; vol. 94, p. 112, deal with the appointment of arbitrators by the holder of a judicial office.

[3] *Ansell* v. *Evans* [1796] 7 T.R. 1.

[4] Russell, *op. cit.*, p. 48.

[5] *Ibid.*, p. 53; *In re Maitland and Glaysher* [1864] 3 H. & C. 442.

[6] A submission which does not come within the Act is revocable at common law and cannot be made irrevocable. This is the rule as to parol submissions (submission in the sense of the authority of an arbitrator, because the agreement to refer is never revocable, and its breach may give rise to an action for damages (Russell, *op. cit.*, p. 48).

The object of this section is to make a submission irrevocable, except by leave, and to make the arbitrators' award in the same way enforceable as before in the case of a submission made a rule of court.

The court, in granting leave to revoke a "submission," *i.e.* the authority of an arbitrator, will exercise its judicial discretion and considerations come in, *e.g.* as whether the proceedings would be prolonged by leave being granted,[1] or whether the application is the means of obtaining an authoritative decision.[2]

Revocation has lost considerable ground since s. 19 of the Arbitration Act provides that an arbitrator may be directed to state a special case during the proceedings on any question of law. Therefore the court will not be induced, except under special circumstances, to give "leave to revoke unless a case is stated."[3] Excess or refusal of jurisdiction by arbitrators or misconduct of arbitrators form the chief grounds for granting leave to revoke. Sometimes revocation may be the only means of preventing a substantial miscarriage of justice, as where an arbitrator received evidence as to claims not within his jurisdiction, and the award could not have been set aside. Misconduct means legal misconduct, as *e.g.* irregularities in proceedings. Disqualification of an arbitrator by interest after his appointment may again be a ground for revocation.[4]

Death of either party before the making of the award revokes in the absence of a contrary provision in the submission, therefore clauses to the contrary are usually inserted into a submission. Bankruptcy does not, of itself, operate as revocation, but it may be sufficient ground for the court to grant leave for the other party to revoke.[5] Another means of defeating a submission for the time being may be by injunction restraining a party from proceeding to arbitration until by separate action the validity of the instrument containing the arbitration clause is determined.[6] This very rare equitable remedy may also be applied to restrain an action in a foreign court in the case of an arbitration clause making the award a condition precedent, when English law was applicable to the contract.[7]

II. By s. 2 of the Arbitration Act, which reads:

> A submission, unless a contrary intention is expressed therein, shall be deemed to include the provisions set forth in the First Schedule of this Act, so far as they are applicable to the reference under the submission.

The provisions of the First Schedule are therefore included, unless a contrary intention is clearly expressed. These provisions will be considered later in their proper place.

[1] *Steamship Den of Airlie & Co., Ltd.* v. *Mitsur & Co. Ltd.* [1912] 106 L.T. 451.
[2] *In re Gerard (Lord) and London & North-Western Rly. Co., Ltd.* [1894] 1 Q.B. 459.
[3] *Tabernacle Permanent Building Society* v. *Knight* [1892] A.C., p. 301.
[4] *In re Baring Bros. and Doulton & Co.* [1892] 61 L.J.Q.B. 704.
[5] *Marsh* v. *Wood* [1829] p B & C. 659.
[6] *Witt* v. *Corcoran* [1871] 8 Ch. App. 476.
[7] *Pena Copper Mines, Ltd.* v. *Rio Tinto Co., Ltd.* [1912] 105 L.T. 846.

Otherwise a submission may contain any provisions the parties desire, unless they are contrary to public policy or oust the jurisdiction of the court.[1] The following provisions were not considered to oust the jurisdiction of the court:

No action shall be brought until an award has been made.[2]

Neither party shall apply to the court to direct the arbitrator to state a special case for the opinion of the court.[3]

The effects of a valid submission are described by s. 4 of the Arbitration Act, which provides:

If any party to a submission, or any person claiming through or under him, commences any legal proceedings in any court against any other party to the submission, or any person claiming through or under him, in respect of any matter agreed to be referred, any party to such legal proceedings may at any time after appearance, and before delivering any pleadings or taking any other steps in the action, apply to that court to stay the proceedings, and that court or judge thereof, if satisfied that there is no sufficient reason why the matter should not be referred in accordance with the submission, and that the applicant was, at the time when the proceedings were commenced, and still remains, ready and willing to do all things necessary to the proper conduct of the arbitration, may make an order staying the proceedings.

Under this section the court has a discretion to stay the proceedings or to try such disputes itself, unless the award was made a condition precedent to an action. In such case the court may as well stay an action, but if the action proceeds, this clause gives a complete defence.[4] The court may also refuse to stay the action where a substantial part of the action does not fall within the submission or where the arbitrator can only decide as to the quantum, but not as to the liability.[5] Also if a case is made out that the contract containing the arbitration clause is repudiated, the court will refuse a stay. Generally the leaning of the court is to stay the action and the burden of showing cause why the action should not be stayed is upon the party opposing the application to stay.[6] The chief grounds for the discretion of the court to refuse to stay an action are, that charges of a personal character are involved, or chiefly questions of law are in dispute or bias of an arbitrator.[7]

In addition to granting a stay, the court may give auxiliary relief, *e.g.* by appointment of a receiver or by granting an injunction.[8]

(*b*) *German Law.*—The submission and its effects under German law are, in comparison with the English rules, of a very simple nature. The agreement to refer to arbitration the so-called *Schiedsvertrag* (see §§ 1026, 1028, *Z.P.O.*) is not defined by German law, but in accordance with the

[1] Russell, *op. cit.*, p. 56.
[2] *Scott* v. *Avery* [1856] 25 L.J. Ex. 308.
[3] *In re Montgomery, Jones & Co. and Liebenthal Co.* [1898] 78 L.T. 406.
[4] *Harrowby* v. *Leicester Corporation* [1915] 85 L.J. Ch. 150.
[5] Russell, *op. cit.*, p. 60.
[6] *Denton* v. *Legge* [1895] 72 L.T. 626.
[7] Russell, *op. cit.*, p. 106.
[8] *Ibid.*, p. 119.

English law it embraces an agreement to refer future or existing disputes to arbitration, whether an arbitrator is named or not (§§ 1025, 1026, 1028, 1031, *Z.P.O.*). The contract may be parol, if it is so valid according to the general rules of the German Civil Code. But a party to a valid parol submission may request the other party to constitute the submission in writing (§ 1027, *Z.P.O.*). This right may be specifically enforced by action.[1] A general agreement to refer future disputes is only valid if it refers to future disputes arising out of a certain and distinct legal relationship between the parties. This is different from English law, where it is possible to refer, as it seems, for the future all matters in difference between the parties.[2]

Where according to the general principles of the German law writing is necessary, *e.g.* §§ 566, 581, B.G.B., it is necessary that the instrument containing the submission should be contained in one signed document; correspondence would seem to be insufficient (126 B.G.B.).[3]

The power of the court under German law to grant leave to revoke a submission is much narrower than under English law. By the rules of the German Civil Code it seems that the authority of an arbitrator is equally revocable as by English law,[4] but by the express provisions of § 1030, *Z.P.O.* a party to a submission is bound as soon as the notification of the appointment of the arbitrator is received by the other party. If the appointment is already contained in the arbitration clause and made by mutual consent of the parties to the submission (§ 1033, *Z.P.O.*) different and even stronger considerations arise (see *infra*). The court, under English law, has power to grant leave to revoke the submission, *i.e.* the authority conferred upon the arbitrator, which revocation in fact although not theoretically invalidates an agreement to refer, and in so doing considerations may be taken into account by the court some of which have nothing at all to do with the person itself of the arbitrator, as *e.g.* legal misconduct, convenience and expense, excess of jurisdiction by arbitrator.

The court, under German law, decides on the application of a party whether a submission is to be revoked or not (§ 1045, *Z.P.O.*), but only such considerations enter into the judicial discretion of the court as are strictly personal to the arbitrator (§ 1032, *Z.P.O.*), and such revocation does not in fact invalidate an agreement to refer (§ 1031, *Z.P.O.*) except where the authority of an arbitrator is revoked who by mutual agreement of the parties was appointed arbitrator in the agreement to refer (§ 1033, *Z.P.O.*), unless the parties have made a provision to the contrary.

Revocation of a submission, *i.e.* the authority of an arbitrator, but not of the agreement to refer arises apart from the decision of a court,

[1] Stein, *op. cit.*, vol. ii, p. 1035.
[2] Russell, *op. cit.*, p. 80.
[3] Under English law correspondence is sufficient if the submission falls within the Statute of Frauds. For the position under German law see also Mittelstein in Nussbaum's *Yearbook*, vol. i, p. 41, and *R.G.*, vol. 68, p. 186.
[4] *R.G.*, Warneyer, 1912, No. 369.

if an arbitrator not appointed by consent in the agreement to refer dies or refuses to become arbitrator or to arbitrate, or is otherwise prohibited. In such case a new arbitrator is to be appointed in his place (§ 1031, *Z.P.O.*).[1] If, however, an arbitrator or arbitrators appointed by consent in the agreement to refer die or refuse to become arbitrators, or rescind their contract to arbitrate, or delay the performance of their duties unduly, or if an even number of arbitrators generally are unable to form a majority, not only the submission, but also the agreement to refer becomes void subject to provisions to the contrary (§ 1033, *Z.P.O.*). To this special class of arbitrators there is nothing corresponding under English law.[2] In practice the parties insert a provision that a third arbitrator is to be appointed, as the German law does not officially recognize an umpire.

The death of a party before the award under English law may best be compared in its effects and the possibility for the parties to provide to the contrary with the annulation of a submission under § 1033, German *Z.P.O.* Under German law death of a party does not affect a submission at all,[3] unless the submission is in respect of personal injuries, as §§ 847, 1300, B.G.B. (*actio personalis moritur cum persona*). Neither does bankruptcy invalidate a submission, although the bankrupt cannot bind his creditors after a receiving order (§ 7, *K.O.*). A submission may also be revoked if the instrument containing the arbitration clause is impeached. But the determination of the legal validity of this instrument by the ordinary courts (§ 1045, *Z.P.O.*) must not interfere and especially not delay the arbitration proceedings, so that an injunction to restrain parties to proceed as under English law never lies by the express provisions of § 1037, *Z.P.O.* The reason is that a revocation of the submission by order of the court even subsequent to an award renders this award ineffective.[4]

As to the contents of the submission there does not exist a "first Schedule," but the provisions of the *Z.P.O.* are applicable, if a submission leaves a gap, where the provisions of the Code provide a solution, as *e.g.* §§ 1028, 1038, *Z.P.O.* Under German law there is no doctrine developed as to the ousting of jurisdiction of the courts,[5] but it seems that parties

[1] The position is similar under ss. 5, 6, Arbitration Act.

[2] Mr. Weiss, in 43 *L.Q.R.*, p. 208, states the position inaccurately because he omits the element of consent in the appointment of the arbitrator named in the submission; see Stein, vol. ii, p. 1042. The underlying idea is that the parties may have referred in reliance on, and confidence in, some special arbitrators. (See also Nussbaum, *Yearbook*, vol. ii, p. 397.)

[3] See Engelmann, *Das Bürgerliche Recht Deutschlands*, 1913, p. 216, §§ 672, 675, B.G.B; Enneccerus Kipp Wolff, *Lehrbuch des Bürgerlichen Rechts*, 1913, vol. i, p. 588; Stein, *op. cit.*, vol. ii, p. 1033 n. 61.

[4] Stein, vol. ii, p. 1076.

[5] Under German law an arbitration clause may be contained in a will (Stein, vol. ii, p. 1078). Under English law such clause would be invalid (*Phillips* v. *Bury* [1695] Skin. 469).

to an arbitration cannot validly renounce their rights to apply to the courts for an injunction.[1]

The courts under German law have no discretion to stay proceedings, but the courts must stay and give judgment for the party who opposes the trial and has made out a case of valid submission (§§ 274, sect. 3, 275, *Z.P.O.*)

The judgment given for the defendant after having proved his objection does not decide the case on its merits, but disposes of it, as far as the courts are concerned, for the time being, until the submission may become void.[2] In broad principles it seems, therefore, that a submission under German law has, as regards "staying proceedings," the same effect as an arbitration clause under English law, which makes arbitration a condition precedent. Under both systems of laws the right to insist on arbitration may be waived by the parties.[3]

Conduct of a Reference.—(*a*) *English Law.*—As to the conduct of arbitration proceedings, which may vary according to the provisions of the submission, we shall consider what rules must be followed, in order to render an award valid, and what rules are provided for by statutes if the submission does not exclude them and does not regulate the procedure itself. In addition we shall have to observe also how far the courts are able to interfere with or influence the arbitration proceedings.

Under English law, if the submission does not contain a provision as to the number and the mode of appointment of the arbitrators, and the First Schedule is not excluded, the reference is to a single arbitrator.[4] If the First Schedule is, however, excluded, and no provisions are contained in the submission, a deadlock arises and in default of written consent the arbitration cannot proceed. If the reference is by application of the First Schedule to a single arbitrator, and the parties do not, after differences have arisen, concur in the appointment of an arbitrator, any party may serve the other party with a written notice to appoint an arbitrator, and if the appointment is not made within seven clear days after the service of the notice the court or a judge may, on application by the party who gave the notice, appoint an arbitrator (s. 50 of the Arbitration Act). The same procedure applies, if the appointed single arbitrator refuses to act or is incapable of acting or dies, unless the submission shows that it was intended that the vacancy should not be supplied[5] (s. 5 (*b*) of the Arbitration Act).

If the reference is to two arbitrators and the First Schedule is not excluded, the two arbitrators may appoint an umpire at any time within the period during which they have power to make an award (the First Schedule (*b*)). If they fail the same procedure as above applies. Notice

[1] Stein, vol. ii, p. 1032; *R.G.*, 30, 322.
[2] *Ibid.*, vol. i, p. 715.
[3] § 274, *Z.P.O.*; *Toronto Rail Co.* v. *National, etc., Insurance Co.* [1914] 20 Com. Cas. 1.
[4] First Schedule (*a*).
[5] This would correspond with the position under German law of an arbitrator appointed by consent in the submission (§ 1033, *Z.P.O.*).

to be served from arbitrator to arbitrator (s. 5 (*c*) Arbitration Act) and the same applies if the appointed umpire refuses to act, etc. (as in s. 5 (*b*) Arbitration Act). But as the two arbitrators have power to appoint an umpire during such time as they have power to make an award, and as they are at liberty to enlarge the time for making an award under clause (*c*) of the First Schedule it would seem that the power of the court to appoint an umpire under s. 5 (*c*) of the Act may become inoperative.[1]

If a submission is to two arbitrators, one to be appointed by each party, and the submission does not express a contrary intention, the party who appointed an arbitrator may appoint a new arbitrator in his place, if the arbitrator refuses to act, or is incapable of acting or dies (s. 6 (*a*) Arbitration Act). But if on a reference to two arbitrators one party fails to appoint an arbitrator, either originally or by way of substitution, the party having appointed his arbitrator may give seven clear days' notice to the other party in default, and after such time, if the appointment is not made, the party who has appointed an arbitrator may appoint that arbitrator to act as sole arbitrator in the reference, provided that the court may set aside any such appointment (s. 6 (*b*) Arbitration Act).

The appointment of an arbitrator under this section is not complete until it has been notified to the other side,[2] and it would seem that the power of the court to set aside an appointment under this section applies only to a sole arbitrator, who, having been set aside as such, remains arbitrator for the party.[3] Where a submission is to three arbitrators, one to be appointed by each party, and the third to be appointed by the two arbitrators, the position is similar (s. 16 of the Administration of Justice Act, 1920, 10 & 11 Geo. V, c. 81). But it is worth mentioning that the court may, on application of a party who served notice upon the arbitrators to appoint the third arbitrator, exercise in the place of the two arbitrators the power of appointing the third arbitrator.

The difference between the position of an umpire and arbitrator is in outline this: The third arbitrator must act together with the other two arbitrators. He must be present at each meeting and witnesses and parties must be examined in the presence of them all,[4] and they should execute the award at the same time and place, and failure to do so may invalidate the award, subject always to the parties not having provided differently. The function of the umpire, however, begins when the functions of the arbitrators cease. Clause (*d*) of the First Schedule provides:

> If the arbitrators have allowed their time or extended time to expire without making an award, or have delivered to any party to the submission or to the umpire a notice in writing, stating that they cannot agree, the umpire may forthwith enter on the reference in lieu of the arbitrators.

[1] Russell, *op. cit.*, p. 130.
[2] Russell, *op. cit.*, p. 139.
[3] *Tew* v. *Harriss* [1848] 11 Q.B. 7.
[4] *Lord* v. *Lord* [1855] 26 L.J.Q.B. 34.

But in practice and in order to save expense and delay it is often arranged[1] that the umpire is to sit with the arbitrators from the commencement of the action, but he is not to interfere at such stage.[2] Otherwise the umpire would have to hear the evidence over again, as in default of consent of both parties he would not be allowed to use the notes of the arbitrators.[3] This is the position, however, where in practice the arbitrators act as counsel, and the umpire acts as sole arbitrator.[4] Sometimes an appeal committee is constituted to hear appeals from the awards of an arbitrator. Such appeal committee is in law considered as an umpire.[5]

By clauses (*f*) and (*g*) of the First Schedule (if not excluded) the arbitrators are empowered to examine the parties, and the witnesses on oath or affirmation, and may require the parties to produce relevant books and papers, etc., within their possession or power. They " are, like other judges, bound, when they are not expressly absolved from doing so, to observe in their proceedings the ordinary rules which are laid down for the administration of justice."[6] They are as a general proposition bound by the rules of evidence,[7] although a not too minute observance of the regularity of forms should be insisted upon.[8] The proceedings bear so much of a judicial character that witnesses can be compelled to attend and are free from arrest.[9] An arbitrator must not hear a party or his witness in the absence of the other party or his representative,[10] and must not receive secret information from one side. The arbitrator has, in the absence of express provision in the submission to the contrary, to decide the questions submitted to him according to the legal rights of the parties, and not according to what he may consider fair and reasonable under the circumstances.[11]

If an arbitrator decides erroneously as to a question of law, but honestly, that is not in itself such misconduct as to set an award aside, unless the improper decision amounts to a miscarriage of justice.[12] In commercial arbitrations, as has already been mentioned, the arbitrators present the evidence to the umpire and act as advocates.

Unless a contrary intention is expressed in the submission the arbitrators or umpire may state an award as to the whole or part of the submission in the form of a special case for the opinion of the Court (s. 7 (*b*) Arbitration Act).

This is in the absolute discretion of the arbitrator or umpire under this section, and refusal does not amount to misconduct. The award stating a special case must set out all the facts necessary for the court to give the

[1] Bacon, *op. cit.*, p. 16.
[2] Russell, *op. cit.*, p. 428.
[3] *In re Jenkins* [1841] 11 L.J.Q.B. 71.
[4] This position is disapproved by Russell, p. 422, quoting cases.
[5] *Keighley, Maxted & Co.* v. *Bryan, Durant & Co.* [1893] 1 Q.B. 405.
[6] *Haigh* v. *Haigh* [1861] 5 L.T. 507.
[7] *In re Enoch and Zaretski, Bock & Co* [1910] 1 K.B. 327.
[8] *Andrews* v. *Mitchell* [1905] A.C. 78.
[9] Russell, *op. cit.*, p. 145.
[10] *Ibid.*, p. 374.
[11] *Ibid.*, p. 376.
[12] *Hagger* v. *Baker* [1845] 14 L.J. Ex. 227; Russell, *op. cit.*, pp. 375, 398.

decision on the point of law, and if the position admits of an alternative decision, the award should be alternative and so final that the court has merely to decide the law in one of the alternatives, whereupon the award of the arbitrator takes effect automatically according to the view adopted by the court.[1] The arbitrators or umpire, after having stated the award in the form of a special case become *functi officio*, but an award may be remitted to them for reconsideration (s. 10 Arbitration Act) when their functions will revive. The special case under this section will be set down for hearing in different ways depending whether it comes on in the King's Bench Division or Chancery Division.[2] By s. 19 of the Arbitration Act " Any referee, arbitrator or umpire may at any stage of the proceedings under a reference, and shall, if so directed by the court or judge, state in the form of a special case for the opinion of the court any question of law arising in the course of the reference." Under this section an arbitrator may be compelled by the court to state a case on application of a party. It is not misconduct for an arbitrator not to state a case provided he gives either party opportunity to make the application to the court.[3]

It seems that the parties may validly stipulate in the submission that the court should not be consulted by way of stating a case, and that this does not oust the jurisdiction of the courts.[4] Also under this section the case has to state the facts on which the decision of the court on points of law is sought. The decision of the court under this section is merely consultative, and the arbitrator has to give his final award according to the court's opinion on the point of law raised. No appeal lies against the opinion of the court as such.

The last power of the court before the making of the award, which we have to consider here, is the power of the court to remove the arbitrator (s. 11–1, Arbitration Act). Ground for removing is his misconduct. What may constitute misconduct we shall deal with later when we have to consider the setting aside of an award for misconduct of an arbitrator. But misconduct such as to give ground for a removing can naturally only be such misconduct as appears before the making of an award.

Finally, the question of time is to be mentioned. If clauses (*c*) and (*e*) of the First Schedule are not excluded the arbitrators must make their award within three months, and the umpire within one month after entering on the reference, but they may both extend the time for making the award by any writing signed by them. This power must, however, be exercised before the expiration of the original period, afterwards only the court can extend the time. (S. 9 Arbitration Act.[5])

(*b*) *German Law.*—We turn now to consider the proceedings from the submission until the making of the award under German law.

If the submission does not contain a provision to the contrary, the

[1] *Larrinaga* v. *Société Franco-Americaine* [1922] 38 T.L.R. 739.
[2] Russell, *op. cit.*, p. 151.
[3] *In re Palmer & Co. and Harkenx & Co.* [1898] 1 Q.B. 131.
[4] Russell, *op. cit.*, p. 316. [5] See also Russell, *op. cit.*, p. 163.

reference is to two arbitrators (§ 1028, *Z.P.O.*) each appointed by a party. A party who has appointed his arbitrator may request the other party in default to appoint an arbitrator within one week from the receipt of the notice in writing to this effect. This notice is also to contain the name of the arbitrator appointed, by the party giving notice (§ 1029, *Z.P.O.*). If the appointment is not made in time, the court is to appoint the arbitrator, on the application of the party not in default (§ 1029, *Z.P.O.*). The power of the court does not arise if the arbitrators are to be appointed by both parties together or by a third person.[1]

A party is bound by the appointment made as soon as notification of the appointment is received by the other party (§ 1030, *Z.P.O.*). It is of importance to note that a notification and request by one party to another to appoint an arbitrator interrupts the running of the period of limitation or prescription (§§ 220, 942, B.G.B.).[2]

Again, we find in § 1031, *Z.P.O.*, similar to the provisions in s. 6 (*a*) of the Arbitration Act, a provision empowering a party to appoint a new arbitrator in the place of an arbitrator who after appointment dies, or became incapable of acting, providing that he was not an arbitrator appointed by consent in the submission. If a party does not appoint a new arbitrator after request, application may be made after a week's time to the court by the other party for the appointment of a new arbitrator. The German law does not officially recognize a third arbitrator or umpire, and provisions for their appointment must be contained in the submission. One observes, also, that the German law makes regulations only in respect of the statutory position of two arbitrators, each to be appointed by a party, but does not provide at all for a single arbitrator and emergencies arising therefrom. In the case of two arbitrators, at variance with English law, the arbitrator is appointed by the court, if a party is in default. If the two arbitrators cannot agree, the submission is revoked (§ 1033, s. 2, *Z.P.O.*). It seems that the underlying idea of the Code is that in a normal case the parties want the case to be decided by arbitrators who have their confidence and appointed by them, *i.e.* by each separately. If these two persons of confidence cannot agree, the probable intention of the parties is to go to court.[3]

[1] *R.G.*, 108, 246. If under English law by the statutory rule (clause (*a*) of First Schedule) the reference is to a single arbitrator and by the submission this arbitrator is to be appointed by a third person, and the arbitrator so appointed refuses to act, then it seems the court has power to make the appointment by virtue of s. 5 (*b*) of the Arbitration Act (Russell, *op. cit.*, p. 127). But it seems that where the third person refuses to appoint, the English court has equally no power to appoint.

[2] Under English and German law a submission may already avoid limitation if the submission is unqualified enough (see Darby and Bosanquet, *Statutes of Limitations*, 1893, p. 100; § 208, B.G.B.). But otherwise, arbitration proceedings will not affect the running of the period of limitation under English law.

[3] This position is very much criticized by Mr. Weiss (43 *L.Q.R.*, p. 208) as a "very extraordinary provision." But the same position occurs in the French *Code de Procédure Civile*, 1612, s. 3, and in the laws of Spain, Japan and Austria. See Nussbaum, *Yearbook*, vol. ii, p. 397. See also footnote 4 on page 20.)

It is therefore usual for the parties to make express provisions as to a third arbitrator in the submission, if they so desire.[1]

When dealing (on p. 69) with the revocation of a submission under German law we have already seen that a valid objection to an arbitrator appointed by consent of the parties in the submission revokes the submission in the same way as disagreement of two arbitrators in default of a provision to the contrary in the submission. We have now to mention the cases of objection to an arbitrator not appointed by consent and/or in the submission. These are the cases nearest approaching to a removal in the meaning of English law. But whereas under English law a removal by the court takes place for misconduct, which includes such a wide ground as the arbitrator's breach of duty to behave fairly to each party and to act within his authority and according to the principles of justice,[2] and the English court may restrain an arbitrator by injunction from acting where he is in the opinion of the court guilty of misconduct,[3] under German law there is no removal in the strict English sense. All the court does upon application is to declare that an arbitrator is validly objected to[4] and only grounds of personal disqualification, such as interest and lack of impartiality, will be taken into consideration (§ 1032, *Z.P.O.*), or unreasonable delay. In addition, the German court has no means of restraining an arbitrator unfit in its opinion to act, but the arbitrators may continue to act, if this should be actually feasible (§ 1047, *Z.P.O.*). The award in such a case would presumably be set aside (§ 1041, s. 1, *Z.P.O.*). There is nothing under German law corresponding to a case or special case stated.

The general position of an arbitrator under German law is like that of a judge, and his judicial and impartial acting is essential.[5] He is liable to the parties for an intentional breach of his duty, *i.e.* malice.[6] It seems that under German law an arbitrator has greater latitude in applying the law than an English arbitrator has,[7] because, according to German law (1042, *Z.P.O.*) the only limits are that an arbitrator does not intentionally deviate from such provisions of the German law as are *jus cogens* and the breach of which could not validly have been waived by the parties. Provisions of this nature in the interest of public policy are, *e.g.*, the rules as to gaming and wager.[8] Such intentional disregard may be presumed if the arbitrator, on hearing arguments, fails to inquire sufficiently. In contrast to the limitations imposed upon the arbitrator under English law the German limitations are confined to those absolutely necessary in the interests of public policy.

Under English law an arbitrator commits misconduct if he intention-

1 See Mittelstein in Nussbaum's *Yearbook*, vol. i, p. 42.
2 Russell, *op. cit.*, p. 204.
3 *Beddow* v. *Beddow* [1878] 9 Ch.D. 89.
4 §§ 1045, 1032, *Z.P.O.*
5 *R.G.*, vol. 94, 212.
6 *R.G.*, vol. 65, p. 175; Stein, *op. cit.*, vol. ii, p. 1044.
7 Russell, *op. cit.*, p. 376.
8 §§ 63, 65, Börsengesetz of May 27, 1908.

ally disregards the law to be applied [1]; under German law an award may be set aside if an arbitrator disregards *jus cogens*. Under German law, in fact, the old English rule of practice, followed when revocation is sought, applies that parties submitting to a reference take the arbitrator with his law good or bad, for better for worse,[2] and it is no miscarriage of justice for a party to be injured by bad law which he has agreed to be bound by.[3] And this, I think, is one of the main reasons why a submission is revoked under the German statutory rule,[4] if two arbitrators of the parties' choice fail to agree.

In regard to the rules of procedure and evidence the parties are in the first instance entitled to make binding provisions in the submission, the breach of which may afterwards cause the award to be set aside, *e.g.* if parties have stipulated that the case should be tried by hearing evidence, and the trial is, notwithstanding that, conducted by writing.[5] But if the parties do not make any provision,[6] the arbitrators have an absolute discretion by law to make their own rules of procedure. They are only limited in one respect: that they must hear both parties before making the award. Failure to comply with this duty may cause the award to be set aside, unless the parties have by consent agreed that this should not be a ground for setting aside the award (§ 1041, s. 4, *Z.P.O.*).[7]

[1] *In re King and Duveen* [1913] 2 K.B. 32. Mr. Weiss writes in 43 *L.Q.R.*, p. 208: " There are few rules dealing with the procedure in an arbitration, but there is, on the other hand, a provision which may fairly be described as a dangerous pitfall. No award shall be enforceable if the arbitrators have disregarded some provision of the law which is *jus strictum* in the sense that the parties cannot provide anything to the contrary (1042, *Z.P.O.*, s. 2). So vague a clause must needs give rise to many doubts, particularly since it seems to compel the arbitrators not only to know the whole substantive law, but also to apply it where necessary, and to apply it correctly." It is clear that modern legislation cannot dispense with " vague " clauses, as Mr. Weiss puts it, or " Generale reservationen." Compare " misconduct " in s. 11 of the Arbitration Act or to act " fairly and properly." I am unable to follow Mr. Weiss's arguments here.

[2] *James* v. *James* [1889] 22 Q.B., p. 674.

[3] *Forwood* v. *Watney* [1880] 49 L.J.Q.B., 447.

[4] § 1033, s. 2, *Z.P.O.*

[5] *R.G.*, vol. 24, p. 397; vol. 47, p. 427.

[6] A reference to a constituted tribunal with fixed rules of procedure includes also these rules (Stein, *op. cit.*, vol. ii, p. 1035, n. 5).

[7] Mr. Weiss writes in 43 *L.Q.R.*, p. 208: The arbitrators " are not, however, bound to follow the ordinary rules of procedure or evidence, and are sometimes even precluded from applying them," and cites in support a decision of the *Reichsgericht*, vol. 31, p. 374. This decision has nothing to do with that question, as it only deals with the issue that, on an interlocutory injunction, if the court orders a plaintiff to bring an action within a certain time the plaintiff must proceed to arbitration within that time, if there is a submission, and the defendant does not lose his right to apply to have the proceedings stayed, if such an order is made. The arbitration tribunal is a court within the meaning of the order, although it would not be empowered to stop the injunction. This case deals, therefore, only with the position and powers of an arbitration tribunal in the system of German courts. There is no instance known to me where the arbitrator is not bound to follow the ordinary rules of procedure, unless it is a question of power. I am unable to follow Mr. Weiss's reasoning.

The arbitrators can examine witnesses, and expert witnesses, but they cannot examine them on oath or compel their appearance. This power can only be exercised by the court on application of a party (§§ 1035, 1036, *Z.P.O.*).

There is no statutory provision under German law as to the time when the award has to be made. But it is provided by § 1032, *Z.P.O.* that unreasonable delay on the side of an arbitrator not appointed by consent of the parties in the submission may be ground for an objection and removal, and unreasonable delay on the side of the arbitrator appointed by consent of the parties in the submission may revoke the submission.[1] In concluding this chapter, and in order to bring German arbitration proceedings within the statutory German rules under some English formula intelligible to English jurists we may define them as follows: They are arbitration proceedings mainly based upon confidence in two appointed arbitrators who have no power to appoint an umpire (exclusion of clause (*b*) of the First Schedule). The submission would expressly provide that no case or special case should be stated by the arbitrators, that the arbitrators should not be bound to decide according to law except the *jus cogens*, that the arbitrators should be absolutely free to make their own rules of procedure, except that they have to hear both parties, and that the parties would not apply for the removal of an arbitrator for misconduct except for personal disqualifications. In the following part of this article we shall consider the nature of the award in the two laws respectively, and how it is enforced, and shall then discuss questions of conflict of laws as to arbitrations.

The Award.—The termination of arbitration proceedings is the award, and we have to consider its nature, form and effects, and the ways and grounds by which it may be impeached under the two systems of law under inquiry.

(*a*) *English Law.*—Clause (*h*) of the First Schedule runs: "The award to be made by the arbitrators or umpire shall be final and binding on the parties, and the persons claiming under them respectively." This provision is merely declaratory of the common law.[2]

The award must be in writing, where the arbitration falls within the provisions of the Arbitration Act, unless clause (*c*) of the First Schedule is excluded. In the case of several arbitrators it must, in the absence of a contrary provision in the submission, be executed by all the arbitrators jointly at the same time and place.[3] The award is valid as soon as it is made, and the law itself does not require publishing. But in order to make the time run within which a motion to set aside the award must be made under Order LXIV, r. 14, publication may become necessary.

[1] Apart from these effects of an unreasonable delay, an action lies against an arbitrator who after having accepted refuses to act or rescinds the contract or delays unreasonably (*R.G.*, vol. 101, p. 392), but there is no specific performance (§ 888, III, 3, *Z.P.O.*). The position is the same under English law (Russell, *op. cit.*, p. 203).

[2] Russell, *op. cit.*, p. 447.

[3] *Ibid.*, p. 448.

But publication is already effected if the arbitrator, after execution of the award, gives notice to the parties that the award is made and ready to be delivered.[1] It is usual and approved by the court that an arbitrator may keep the award until his fees are paid by the party taking it up.[2] An award does not require technical language as long as it is clear and certain.[3]

" A valid award on a voluntary reference is a final and conclusive judgment, as between the parties, respecting all the matters referred by the submission. It binds the rights of the parties for all time without appeal, both as to fact and law." [4] A party is bound to take notice of an award and to obey it.[5] If an action is brought on a cause which had already been determined by an award, the award is a complete defence by itself, unless an award imposes also a duty, in which case performance of the duty must also be pleaded.[6] A valid award is conclusive evidence as between the parties as to the facts found by it,[7] but not in criminal proceedings.

An award may be set aside where an arbitrator or umpire has misconducted himself, or an arbitration or award has been improperly procured (s. 11, 2, Arbitration Act). Cases of misconduct under this section may arise, where an arbitrator intentionally disregards the law or attempts to preclude a party from an application for a special case to be stated under s. 19 of the Arbitration Act or does not follow the opinion of the court on a case stated under s. 19 of the Arbitration Act, or has some personal interest in the subject-matter of the arbitration, etc.[8]

An award is improperly procured if an arbitrator is bribed or treated or misled by either party by fraudulent concealment of matters where a party was under a duty to disclose. Besides this statutory jurisdiction the court had and has an inherent jurisdiction to set aside awards, if upon the face of the award it can be clearly shown that the arbitrator decided wrongly [9] as to fact or law, unless the error is immaterial for the decision. " Upon the face of the award " includes a document contemporaneously delivered with the award.[10] An award may further be set aside for want of finality [11] as to all subject-matters of the arbitration, or for uncertainty,[12] or if the performance of an award is impossible by its nature or the award inconsistent [13] or in excess of authority. These are not the only grounds for which the court may set aside an award under its inherent jurisdiction, but they are apparently the main ones. If part only of the award is bad and this part is separable, the residue of the award may be good.

[1] Russell, *op. cit.*, p. 452.
[2] *Hicks* v. *Richardson* [1797] 1 B. & P. 93.
[3] *Stonehewer* v. *Farrar* [1845] 6 Q.B. 730.
[4] Russell, *op. cit.*, p. 479. [5] *Ibid.*, p. 487. [6] *Ibid.*, p. 492.
[7] *Ibid.*, p. 494. [8] *Ibid.*, p. 204 ss.
[9] *Buerger* v. *Barnett* [1919] 89 L.J.K.B. 161.
[10] *Halgate* v. *Killick* [1861] 31 L.J. Ex. 7.
[11] Russell, *op. cit.*, p. 220. [12] *Ibid.*, p. 230. [13] *Ibid.*, p. 235.

By order LXIV, r. 14, the application to set aside an award may be made within six weeks after the award has been published to the parties, *i.e.* notice to the parties that the award is made and complete,[1] but the court may extend the time before or after the same has elapsed. It is not intended to deal here with the technical rules of procedure in a motion to set aside an award. As grounds of opposition to a motion to set aside may be preferred,[2] that the party moving was not injured or the party moving acquiesced in the award by knowingly accepting a benefit under it. On a motion to set aside the court may turn the motion into a special case, or refer the award back for reconsideration.[3] In the King's Bench Division the motion is to a Divisional Court and in Chancery to a judge, and an appeal lies to the Court of Appeal.[4]

(*b*) *German Law.*—Under German law the effects of a valid award are the same as under the declaratory provision in clause (*h*) of the First Schedule to the Arbitration Act. § 1040, *Z.P.O.*, reads: "An award has as between the parties the same effects as a valid judgment of a court, against which no appeal lies."

This implies by reference to the effects of a valid judgment of a court all the essential requirements and effects of an ordinary judgment as they are established under German law. So it is necessary that the whole differences in dispute are adjudicated upon by the award and not only elements of it[5] nor interlocutory awards; further that an award is only binding as to the matters referred to arbitration.[6] An award is to be construed and interpreted according to the German rules applying to judgments[7] and reference is to be made to the reasons attached to the award (§ 1041, s. 5, *Z.P.O.*), which seems to correspond with the English practice as to "contemporaneous documents." An award like a German judgment does not bar a new action in the identical dispute, but it is a complete defence, if pleaded. The position is the same as under English law. An award under German law binds not only the parties[8] but all persons claiming through or under them and such third persons or strangers to the submission as can be bound by contracts of the parties. A valid award is conclusive evidence as between the parties on the point decided, but not in criminal matters (§ 262, *Strafprosessordnung*). As to the form of the award § 1039, *Z.P.O.* provides that the award is to be dated and signed by all the arbitrators and signed copies thereof are to be served on the parties, and finally the original, together with proof of service, is to be filed with the clerk of the proper court.

Only after fulfilment of all these requirements does the arbitration

[1] *Hemsworth* v. *Brian* [1844] 14 L.J.C.P. 36.
[2] Russell, *op. cit.*, p. 256 ss.
[3] *Goddard* v. *Smith* [1865] 13 L.T. 159.
[4] Russell, *op. cit.*, p. 263.
[5] Stein, *op. cit.*, vol. i, p. 853.
[6] By analogy of § 322, *Z.P.O.* The position under English law is identical, Russell, *op. cit.*, p. 480.
[7] *R.G.*, vol. 93, p. 156.
[8] Stein, *op. cit.*, vol. ii, p. 1054. Identical English law: Russell, *op. cit.*, p. 485.

come to an end and the arbitrators become *functi officio*. Under English law, as we have seen, there is nothing corresponding to this formal termination of the arbitration, and the publishing there necessary to start the running of the time within which a motion to set aside must be made is of less formality. All the arbitrators have to sign the award, whereas it is sufficient that one of them or a third person file it as agents. The requirements of § 1039, *Z.P.O.* cannot be dispensed with by the parties or arbitrators if a formally legal and valid award is wanted.[1] And these provisions apply equally to German and foreign awards. If the submission does not provide to the contrary the absolute majority of the votes of the arbitrators shall be a sufficient majority (§ 1038, *Z.P.O.*).

In the case of clerical errors and accidental slips appearing on the face of an award the arbitrators may rectify it under observance of the provisions of § 1039, *Z.P.O.*[2]; in case of an award dealing only with part of the subject-matter referred to arbitration the parties may ask the arbitrators to resume their office and deal with the omitted part of the submission.[3]

Under German law an award may be set aside on the grounds enumerated in § 1041, *Z.P.O.* These are:

(1) If the arbitration proceedings were impeachable. This includes cases[4] where the arbitrators had no authority at all to arbitrate, and

[1] Mr. Weiss writes in 43 *L.Q.R.*, p. 206: "As an instance [of the rules of procedure adopted by permanent courts of arbitration displacing the rules of the code] may be mentioned the almost universal disregard of the provision in the Code that every award must be lodged with the court of law, as a condition precedent to proceedings for its enforcement being taken. Indeed, the trade associations, etc., even provided their own sanctions for disobedience to the awards of their courts, of the strongest, and, with respect, the most illegal of which being the blacklisting of the disobedient party. This was, of course, a glaring instance of injustice in that the disobedient party was subjected to arbitrary force regardless of the provisions of the law of the land and the remedies provided by it. That such a state of affairs could not be termed otherwise than as highly objectionable is obvious, and the courts of law have consequently always viewed awards with suspicion."

I am unable to see how the alleged unlawful procedure of trade associations can be disobedience to the provisions of the Code or "displace them." The position is merely this, that a person who does not comply with rules given for his benefit, or does not cause them to be complied with, cannot avail himself of the benefit which the law otherwise would confer. (See also Nussbaum, *Yearbook*, vol. ii, p. 385.) Mr. Weiss is further incorrect in stating that the blacklisting of a disobedient party by a trade association is "most illegal." It is not illegal in England (see *Ware and De Freville, Ltd.* v. *Motor Trade Association*, 37 T.L.R. 213 [1921] 3 K.B. 40, and *Sorrell* v. *Smith* 41 T.L.R. 529 [1925] A.C. 700). By the former case it is even not illegal as against non-members. It is certainly not against German law, if the rules of a trade association are observed. I further fail to see how the courts, in consequence of awards which never came before their tribunal by their nature, could view awards with suspicion.

[2] Stein, *op. cit.*, vol. ii, p. 1051, N. 10. This corresponds with the position under English law by s. 7c of the Arbitration Act.

[3] Under English law an award may be set aside as not final if it does not decide all the issues (*Kilburn* v. *Kilburn* [1845] 13 M. & W. 671).

[4] Stein, *op. cit.*, vol. ii, p. 1057 ss.

cases where they exceeded their authority conferred upon them either by the submission or by the subsidiary provisions of the German law. The former case refers to a submission void *ab initio*, or a submission revoked, or an award deciding disputes not referred, or an arbitrator not properly appointed or properly objected to before the award. The latter case has in view excess of authority by breaking material rules of procedure prescribed by the parties, or an award illegal upon its face or intentional disregard by the arbitrators of those rules of law which are compulsory.[1]

(2) If the performance of the award would be against a rule of law. In case of change by legislation after an award, the law in force at the time of the decision of the court prevails.[2]

(3) If a party was not represented in accordance with the law during the proceedings. This includes cases of an unauthorized agent, and cases where the party had not the legal capacity or right of disposal. But these irregularities may be waived, if possible, by law.

(4) If the right of audience was refused to a party.

(5) If the award has not the reasons annexed.

(6) If a judgment of a court could be upset for the reasons enumerated in § 580 x. 1–6, *Z.P.O.* These reasons are mainly perjury or corrupt practice by a party, witness or judge, or a faked document put in evidence, if the judgment is based upon them and the wrongful acts have been properly proved before a criminal court (§ 581, *Z.P.O.*).

Generally the parties can waive by agreement beforehand their objection to the irregularities under ss. 4 and 5 above, And it would seem that the parties during the arbitration proceedings must object, at the risk of losing their remedy, to irregularities, otherwise the inference may be drawn that a new submission covering the irregularity has been made.[3]

The form of the proceedings to set aside an award is by § 1044, *Z.P.O.* The action must be brought within one month after acquiring knowledge of the irregularity, but this time starts to run at the earliest from the moment an order for the enforcement of an award (see later) becomes unappealable. An action to set aside cannot be brought after ten years from the last-mentioned point of time. If an award is set aside the enforcement of the order is to be revoked at the same time. The

[1] For this last reason a party may also oppose the enforcement of an award, (§ 1042, *Z.P.O.*).

[2] *R.G.*, vol. 108, p. 140.

[3] *R.G.*, vol. 105, p. 385. Under English law this inference cannot be drawn because of the formal requirements of a submission under the Act, but the English court in its discretion may refuse an application on the ground of acquiescence. "What right had he then to lie by, with his grievance dormant in his own bosom, and now dispute, for the first time, the validity of the authority which has been exercised?" (*Bignall* v. *Gale* [1841] 10 L.J.C.P. 169; see Russell, *op. cit.*, pp. 433–36). But under both laws it makes a difference whether the parties appeared themselves or not. German law: *R.G.*, vol. 40, p. 401. For the English law: Russell, *op. cit.*, p. 437.

intention of the German code seems to be to give a party time for his action to set aside an award until the other side has, by obtaining an enforcement order of the court, clearly indicated his intention to avail himself of the benefit of the award. The above grounds for setting aside an award are also available by way of defence in an action for a declaratory judgment, that an award is valid, or in an action brought on the cause after the plaintiff has pleaded the award as reply to the defence taken by the defendant.[1] After an award is set aside the submission, as a rule, comes to an end,[2] except probably where a party was not properly represented in the proceedings (§ 1041, s. 3, *Z.P.O.*).

If we turn now to a comparison of the "setting aside an award" procedure under both systems of law, the following conclusions may be drawn.

All the reasons for which under German law an action to set aside may be brought are reasons on which an English court may either, under s. 11, rule 2 of the Arbitration Act or under its inherent jurisdiction set aside an award except that default in annexing the reasons to an award under English law does not affect an award unless the parties have provided differently in the submission. On the other hand, the grounds for setting aside under English law are wider as they include intentional disregard of all rules of law and a wrong decision of the arbitrator appearing on the face of the award. The procedure under English law is more elastic and gives room for the discretion of a court to turn the motion into a special case or to refer back, whereas the German court has no such discretion. Finally, there is under English law a ground of defence to a motion to set aside, namely that the party seeking the relief was not injured, which is unknown to German law.

Enforcement of the Award.—The last chapter of our inquiry, moving on comparative lines, is on the enforcement of awards.

(*a*) *English Law.*—Under English law an award may be enforced in the following ways:

(1) By action as of right, whether the submission was by parol, by writing under hand or by deed. This action is based upon an implied mutual promise in the submission to perform the award of the arbitrator.[3]

The enforcement by action is the appropriate remedy where a submission is by parol or where an award is not final or where the validity of an award is doubtful. The action is not precluded by a prior order under s. 12 of the Arbitration Act or by a prior committal for contempt. The claim is based on the submission and the award. Only such defences are available as are directed against the submission and the validity of the award, therefore error of facts, misconduct or mistake[4] on the part of the arbitrator cannot be pleaded in this action, but the proper course would be in respect of them to move to have the award set aside.

[1] Stein, *op. cit.*, vol. ii, p. 1055.
[2] *R.G.*, vol. 108, p. 374; vol. 69, p. 54.
[3] Russell, *op. cit.*, p. 273.
[4] *Thorburn* v. *Barnes* [1867] L.R. 2 C.P. 384.

But accord and satisfaction and excess of jurisdiction are a good defence.[1]

(2) An award may be enforced by attachment. By s. 1 of the Arbitration Act a submission has the same effect as if it had been made an order of court. Therefore the old procedure of attachment still lies in this case, although it does not extend any more to debts of money (Debtors Act, 1869, s. 4). The submission must be in writing, if an attachment should be sought for. Attachment is the penal process of arrest and imprisonment for contempt of court. A party, in order to succeed on a motion for attachment, must prove that the award had been served upon the other party, and that a demand had been made to obey the award. Such a motion may be opposed by objections as to irregularities in the demand, or service, or defects on face of the award, or revocation of submission, or it may be pleaded that a condition precedent has not been performed, or that the validity of the award is doubtful. The court, in granting an attachment, may stay it for a certain period or impose such terms as would seen equitable.[2] Attachment is rare since the Arbitration Act.

(3) The courts by their inherent jurisdiction could always give a rule for the payment of the amount awarded, and since the Judgments Act, 1883 (1 & 2 Vict., c. 110), s. 18 such a rule has the effect of a judgment. The power to grant a rule is discretionary. A rule to pay the amount awarded is not of importance or advantage now since

(4) S. 12 of the Arbitration Act provides a better mode. It runs: "An award on a submission may, by leave of the Court or a judge, be enforced in the same manner as a judgment or order to the same effect."

The submission, to fall under this section, must be in writing. The application of a party to the court under this section is to ask that judgment may issue on the award. The court has, however, no power to direct judgment to be entered in accordance with an award,[3] because this would be a judgment instead of leave to enforce an award. A party may bring an action on the award notwithstanding that leave to enforce had been obtained.[4] But leave to enforce will not be granted and an action on the award instead is to be preferred where an award is not final, as where it omits to define the liability[5] or where the validity of an award is doubtful.[6] After leave has been obtained, the ordinary rules as to execution of judgments apply (Order 42 of the Rules of the Supreme Court). Writs of execution are issued for the High Court at the Central Office (O. 61, r.l.n.) and the order of the court and the award are to be produced to the officer by whom the writ should be issued (O. 42, r. 10).

[1] Russell, *op. cit.*, pp. 282, 283 ss. [2] *Ibid.*, p. 304. [3] *Ibid.*, p. 268.
[4] *China Steam Navigation Co.* v. *Van Laun* [1905] 22 T.L.R. 26.
[5] *In re Willesden Local Board and Wright* [1896] 2 Q.B. 412.
[6] *In re Boks & Co. and Peters, Rushton & Co.*, 120 L.T. 516.

(*b*) *German Law.*—Under German law the modes of enforcing an award are fewer; (1) § 1042, *Z.P.O.* runs as follows: "Execution may issue on an award if the award has been declared enforceable by decree of the court."

"The decree is not to be granted if the award intentionally disregards rules of law, which the parties could not validly have dispensed with. The motion for a decree is to be stayed if a party has proved within a period fixed by the court that he has brought an action to set aside the award."

The decision of the court is in the form of a "decree," which implies, in the German legal language, that a hearing is not required, but a pleading in writing is sufficient, and the decree does not need to have the reasons annexed (§ 329, *Z.P.O.*).

There is further no appeal in the technical sense against decrees, but only a *Beschwerde*, or rather *sofortige Beschwerde* as provided for by § 1045, *Z.P.O.*

The intention of the code is to simplify the proceedings for obtaining a decree of leave to enforce and not to hear any objections to an award in these proceedings, but to have them referred to a proper action to set aside an award, except where it is alleged and proved that the arbitrators intentionally disregarded some of the few compulsory rules of law, which are given for reasons of German public policy. It is obvious that no court can give its assistance to enforce awards labouring under such intentional disregard on the side of the arbitrators. And this exception must also be extended to cases where the performance of the award would be against a rule of law.[1] Otherwise, an action to set aside an award, and a motion for a decree of leave to enforce, are so much independent, that leave to enforce does not preclude a party afterwards from bringing an action to set aside an award and that leave to enforce has no effect on the validity of an award. The only connecting points are, that a motion to obtain a decree for leave to enforce must be stayed, if a party chooses to bring an action to set aside an award during the proceedings of the motion, which he is on the other hand not bound to do at this stage, and the other connexion is, that the time for the limitation of the action to set aside an award starts to run only after the decree for leave to enforce. Furthermore, as we have seen already, a valid award does not need a decree for leave to enforce in order to have its effects as *res judicata* or as a judgment. But under English law, as we have seen, in the course of a motion for leave to enforce the defendant may plead all the grounds which would render the validity of the award or the right to proceed upon it doubtful, and the English court then usually leaves the parties to proceed by action, and no summary order of leave to enforce will be made.[2] And further, under English law, default in pleading these grounds in the course of a motion may even preclude a party later on from applying to set aside an award on these grounds,

[1] *R.G.*, vol. 108, p. 140.

[2] See note 6, p. 27.

as it may constitute an admission.[1] The present position under English law seems to be the same as it was under German law before the amendment by the Statute of February 13, 1924. Under the old § 1042, *Z.P.O.* a party had in the course of a motion for an execution judgment (as it then was) to plead at the risk of preclusion all the then available grounds for setting aside an award.

After a decree of leave to enforce has been obtained the ordinary procedure for execution on judgments applies, and it is necessary that the clerk of the proper court grants an execution clause (§ 724, *Z.P.O.*) which roughly corresponds with the English institution of writs.

If an award is set aside after a decree of leave to enforce, the decree is to be set aside at the same time (§ 1044, *Z.P.O.*).

If after an award new material has matured which would otherwise be a ground for setting aside an award, this material cannot be brought in a motion for leave to enforce as defence,[2] nor can the award be set aside, but a separate action has to be taken with the purpose of obtaining a judgment of the court declaring that execution will not lie in future on the award (§ 767, *Z.P.O.*).

This action may be brought either before a decree of leave to enforce has been granted or after such a decree. The judgment of a court in this action preserves formally the award, but in fact, execution cannot be levied after such declaratory judgment,[3] and the new material may be used by way of defence against the pleading of an award. So the enforcement of an award in a wider sense is refused.

Under English law discovery of new material or new evidence would in the absence of fraud or concealment not be a good ground either for setting aside an award, but the court would in its discretion remit the award to the arbitrator for reconsideration.[4] And in the course of a motion for leave to enforce the pleading of new material or evidence would result in the refusal of leave to enforce, and in a subsequent action on the award, in which *e.g.* accord and satisfaction[5] may be pleaded.

In concluding our comparison between the German motion for a decree of leave to enforce (§ 1042, *Z.P.O.*) and the English motion for leave to enforce under s. 12 of the Arbitration Act we may well hold that the English motion is an *Exequatur* on the merits of an award in the negative sense, because the court will, in cases of doubt, leave the parties

1 But if a party under English law by voluntary act performs an award this does not seem to constitute acquiescence, and a bar from moving subsequently to have it set aside; see *Bartle* v. *Musgrave* [1841] 1 Dowl. N.S. 325. Order 42 r. 31*a* gives the court discretion to grant leave to enforce, although the time for moving to set aside has not elapsed, and on such terms as may be just.

2 Stein, *op. cit.*, vol. ii, p. 1068.

3 *Ibid.*, p. 528.

4 *Sprague* v. *Allen* [1899] 15 T.L.R. 150.

5 *Smith* v. *Trowsdale* [1854] 3 E. & B. 83.

to their remedy by action on the award, whereas the German motion since the amending Statute of 1924 is in principle an *Exequatur* not on the merits of the award.[1]

(2) The other method of enforcing an award is by action. The action may either be on the award and submission as *causa*, like the English action,[2] or it may be an indirect way of enforcing an award by suing upon the original *causa* and pleading the award by way of reply to defences met by the award.[3] An award so pleaded cannot be defeated by grounds other than would have been available in an action to set aside an award or in the case of new material or facts arising after an award in an action according to § 767, *Z.P.O.*

The action may be brought for two ends. It may either be for the purpose of obtaining a declaratory judgment that an award is valid, and this is possible so far as in general declaratory judgments (§ 256, *Z.P.O.*) may be obtained, *i.e.* if there is a legal interest in an early judicial declaration of the rights. And in the particular instance of an award the justification may also be since the Statute of 1924 in the fact that a motion to set aside an award may be brought after a decree of leave to enforce was obtained. The other form of action is one brought for the performance of the award. According to the general principles of the law of German procedure,[4] it is not open for a claimant to frame his claim as he chooses, but he must adopt the shortest and least expensive mode, if there are two or more ways. This is a principle of economy in procedure, and default of complying with it will lead to a dismissal of an action for "want of protectionable interest."[5] Therefore, success is usually refused to an ordinary action to enforce a German award, because there is the shorter and cheaper way of § 1042, *Z.P.O.* by way of motion for leave to enforce. But under exceptional circumstances an action may be brought on an award where this shorter way is not possible, as in cases of foreign awards, which do not comply with the requirements of German law, and where enforcement of German awards is sought for or against successors in title[6] or where an action for a declaratory judgment would otherwise lie and the action for performance would be the shorter way as against a declaratory judgment, and a subsequent motion for a decree of leave to enforce[7] or where an award is only

[1] The position is similar under s. 15 of the Indian Arbitration Act, 1899, but different under Order 52, s. 3 (14) of the Supreme Court of the Gold Coast Ordinance, No. 4 of 1876.

[2] Stein, *op. cit.*, vol. ii, p. 1065 Note 26.

[3] See Stein, *op. cit.*, vol. ii, p. 1062. Mr. Weiss in 43 *L.Q.R.*, p. 209, calls such an action, not quite correctly, "proceedings *de novo.*" See Nussbaum, *Yearbook*, vol. ii, p. 385. Mr. Weiss mentions only this way by action.

[4] See *e.g. R.G.*, vol. 88, p. 267; and § 256, *Z.P.O.*

[5] See also Kahn, "English judgments *in Personam* and *in Rem* in Germany," *Journal of Comparative Legislation and International Law*, Third Series, vol. ix, pt. iv, p. 218.

[6] Stein, *op. cit.*, vol. ii, p. 1068.

[7] *Ibid.*, p. 1062.

declaratory, and the performance of an obligation arising out of the award is sought.[1]

The *Reichsgericht*,[2] in expressing these principles, says: "An action to enforce an award may be allowed just as well in the case of a German award as in the case of a foreign award, but only if there are obstacles in the way of their being enforced by decree of leave to enforce, which obstacles cannot be remedied, as *e.g.* non-compliance with the provisions of § 1039, *Z.P.O.*" (so apparently also *dicta* in the decision *R.G.*, vol. 30, p. 370, which dealt with the enforcement of foreign awards).

In the subsequent reasons for the above decision the *Reichsgerichts* introduces also a new aspect of the undesirability of an action to enforce a German valid award, because it says the judgment debtor may then be exposed to execution on two titles: the judgment in the action, and the award declared enforceable.[3]

Questions of International Law and Conflict of Laws.—The remaining part of the inquiry must now be directed to the questions of international law and conflict of laws under both systems of law.

(*a*) *English Law.*—Under English law a submission to arbitration under foreign law is valid.[4] The Arbitration Act does not mention foreign awards at all nor does the Common Law define what is a foreign award. It seems that arbitration to be held according to foreign law certainly constitutes a foreign award; it is doubtful, however, whether an arbitration to be held according to English law but in a foreign country would result in an English award. The question is not of great importance, as the arbitration takes place as a rule in England if English law is applicable.

Whether foreign law is to be applied depends upon the intention of the parties to be gathered from the circumstances of the case. Very often the fact that a permanent institution is to function as arbitrator or umpire will indicate whether the arbitration should proceed under foreign or English law, and may have even the further effect of not only making

[1] *Die Rechtsprechung der Oberlandesgerichte*, vol. 29, p. 291. See also Warneyer's *Jahrbuch der Entscheidungen*, 1914, p. 94, No. 70, cited by F. Oppenheimer in Nussbaum, *Yearbook*, vol. i, p. 289 s. These decisions are before the Statutory Amendment of 1924.

[2] Judgment of July 1, 1927, in *Juristische Wochenschrift*, 1927, p. 2464.

[3] These considerations are unknown to English law, as an action may be brought on the award after leave to enforce under s. 12 of the Arbitration Act has been obtained (*China Steam Navigation Co.* v. *Van Laun* [1905] 22 T.L.R. 26). This danger is evidently still greater in the case of a foreign judgment; see W. Piggott, *Foreign Judgments*, vol. i, p. 14. He suggests, as an essential condition for an execution judgment, proof that proper attempts to obtain satisfaction in the country of the first judgment have been made, and that such attempts have failed.

[4] *Merrifield, Ziegler & Co.* v. *Liverpool Cotton Association, Ltd.*, L.T.R. 105, p. 97; *Norske Atlas Insurance Co.* v. *London General Insurance Co.*, 43 T.L.R. 541; *Bankers and Shippers Insurance Co. of New York* v. *Liverpool Marine and General Insurance Co., Ltd.* [1924] 19 Lloyds Law List Reports 335 and 24, p. 85; and see Russell, *op. cit.*, p. 273.

the arbitration clause to be construed and governed by that law,[1] but also the whole contract[2] containing the clause.

The English courts give effect to a submission under foreign arbitration by staying proceedings in an English court, if such should be brought in breach of the contract contained in the submission.[3] This extends to cases of submissions under a foreign court, which is treated for this purpose like an arbitration tribunal.[4] On the other hand, if an action is brought in a foreign country contrary to a submission making the award a condition precedent and to be governed by English law, the court may by injunction restrain a party from pursuing the action.[5] By the Arbitration Clauses (Protocol) Act, 1924 (14 & 15 Geo. V, c. 39), clause 4, it seems that the discretion of the English courts as to granting stay of proceedings is taken away within the limited sphere of the application of the Act.[6] A question of not merely theoretical interest is whether an agreement to refer and the relations arising hereunder are substantive law or deal with the remedy only according to the English conception.

The importance of the distinction lies in the fact that the English courts cannot apply foreign law of procedure or law as to remedies, but only their own, whereas foreign substantive law will be applied, if applicable to a contract. In Hamlyn & Co., etc. (see note 1) it was argued that an *agreement* to refer dealt with the remedy, and was therefore as to its validity subject to the *lex fori*, but Lord Watson said: "I can find no authority, and none was cited to us, to the effect that, in dealing with the prejudicial question, whether the court has jurisdiction to try the merits of the case, the court ought to disregard an agreement to refer which is *pars contractus*, and binding according to the law of the contract, because it would not be valid if tested by the *lex fori*." In the Norske case (see note 4, p. 31) the court, held by applying Norwegian law to the form of a submission in an action on a Norwegian award, that the form of a submission is part of substantive law, and therefore, although the contract in question would not have been admissible as evidence in an action on a policy of reinsurance as being against the *lex fori* (Stamp Act, 1891, s. 93, and Marine Insurance Act, 1906, ss. 22 and 23), it was held admissible as evidence for the submission. In the Merrifield, Ziegler Co. Case (see note 4, p. 31) the question whether in an action on an award a party was authorized to be plaintiff after an assignment of the benefit of an award, was decided according to the *lex fori* because it was held to be a question of procedure.

[1] *Hamlyn & Co.* v. *Talisker Distillery Co.* [1894] A.C. 202, per Lord Herschell at p. 208: "that particular stipulation," namely the arbitration clause, shall be interpreted according to English law.

[2] *Spurrier* v. *La Cloche* [1902] A.C. 446, per Lord Lindley, p. 450.

[3] *The "Dawlish"* [1910] P. 339.

[4] *Kirchner & Co.* v. *Gruben* [1909] 1. Ch. 413; *The "Cap Blanco"* [1913] P. 130.

[5] *Pena Copper Mines, Ltd.* v. *Rio Tinto Co., Ltd.* [1912] 105. L.T. 846.

[6] Dicey, *Conflict of Laws*, 4th ed., p. 364; Ralph Sutton, in Nussbaum's *Yearbook*, vol. i, p. 65.

It seems that the agreement to refer is in respect of questions relating to its validity, considered substantive law or *lex contractus*, whereas the enforcement of an award deals with the law of remedy, and is, therefore, law of procedure.[1]

As to the rules governing the effects of a submission and the conduct of an arbitration it seems that they belong to the law of procedure. "The law having asserted its jurisdiction over these consensual arrangements for the decision of disputes between parties, and the machinery of the law having been introduced which gives effect to them beyond that given by the mere agreement of the parties, the proceedings must be treated on the same footing for the present purposes as proceedings in litigation."[2]

In a case which was brought on appeal from the courts in Madras to the Privy Council the Privy Council confirmed the view taken by Coutts Trotter J., who declined to entertain proceedings brought in Madras to upset an English award. The learned judge said, "How a judge in Madras is supposed to have jurisdiction to upset an award made by an arbitrator in London passes my comprehension, and it is perfectly clear that the court which is given jurisdiction by the English Act is the English court."[3]

The conclusion is that the rules of law governing the effects of a submission and providing also for the supervision of the courts seem to be from the English point of view rules of procedure exclusively to be applied by the English courts and giving the English courts exclusive jurisdiction, so that no other court can apply them, nor may validly apply their own. The court "will also remember that the parties may have agreed to the submission precisely because of the discretionary power thus vested in the court. They may very well have said to themselves, 'If in any particular case it would be unfair to allow the arbitration to which we are agreeing to proceed, we shall have the protection of the court.'"[4] And *vice versa* the English courts would, on the view taken in Oppenheim & Co. (see note 3), be unable to apply their own law of procedure to foreign submissions. These conclusions must, however, necessarily be confined to the effects of a submission. Where, however, the enforcement of an award is concerned these conclusions, of necessity, cannot apply, as each country has to apply here its own law of procedure, whether foreign or its own awards are concerned. In an English action to enforce a foreign award pleas may be taken to defeat the effects of a foreign award on grounds arising under the foreign law governing the award[5] or under English law, as *e.g.* the Statute of Limitations, and accord and satisfaction.

[1] See Nussbaum, in his *Yearbook*, vol. i, pp. 16–17, for general preparation.

[2] Per Collins M.R. in *Croasdell* v. *Cammell Laird & Co., Ltd.* [1906] 2. K.B. 569.

[3] *Oppenheim Co.* v. *Mahamed Haneef* [1922] A.C. 1. 487. The same attitude is taken by German courts (see later).

[4] Ralph Sutton in Nussbaum's *Yearbook*, vol. i, p. 58, dealing with the court's discretion to grant a stay of proceedings.

[5] *In re Bankers and Shippers Insurance Co.*, etc.; see note 4, p. 31.

If there is an arbitration clause under English law in a contract between an English firm and a foreigner, the English court has on application for the appointment of arbitrators under s. 5 of the Act an absolute discretion in dealing with that application and can attach any reasonable condition as to security and costs for the granting of the application.[1] If a party against whom it is sought to enforce an award is out of the jurisdiction it seems that an action on the award was the only proper remedy.[2] Since 1920, by Order XI, r. 8*a* of the Supreme Court service out of the jurisdiction of any summons, etc., to remit, set aside or enforce an award is possible, if the award is made in an arbitration held within the jurisdiction, and it would seem therefore probable that an award may be enforced by the Arbitration Act against persons out of the jurisdiction by the remedies provided.

(*b*) *German Law.*—Under German law a submission to arbitration under foreign law is valid, and generally an action lies to enforce a foreign award.[3] The German *Z.P.O.* does not mention foreign awards nor define them, and it seems that a definition is of little importance for the same reasons as advanced under English law, because the conduct of a reference in Germany will be almost conclusive as to the application of German law to the submission. Otherwise the general principle as to the finding of the proper law applicable to a submission is that the intention of the parties as indicated by the surrounding circumstances is the deciding element.[4] It has been suggested by a German legal writer of authority,[5] in finding the law applicable to a submission, to make the starting-point from the logical *prius*, *i.e.* the award to be made, as submission and award must necessarily follow the same law. So if a permanent institution of a country is made arbitrator, or an award is to be made in a certain country by the provisions of a submission, it would follow that the laws of that country are applicable to the submission. This was the method of the German *Reichsgericht* in a recent decision, where a Strassburg institution was made arbitrator.[6] The same method had also been applied by the English court in the Norske case (see note 4, p. 31). A German court must stay the proceedings or technically refuse an action, if a valid foreign submission is pleaded by way of defence, and it could not exercise the discretion of the English courts, where an English submission is in question, because this is clearly part of the law of procedure, and therefore inapplicable as *lex fori*. It seems that also under German law a foreign

[1] *Bjornstadt* v. *Ouse Shipbuilding Co.* [1924] 2 K.B. 673.

[2] Russell, *op. cit.*, p. 273.

[3] *R.G.*, vol. 30, p. 368 ss., and Entscheidung des R.G. of December 22, 1911, in Teuffert's *Archiv für Entscheidungen der Obersten Gerichte*, vol. 67, p. 426, copied in Nussbaum's *Yearbook*, vol. i, p. 276.

[4] *R.G.*, vol. 30, p. 371.

[5] Jonas, editor of the last edition of Stein's commentary on *Z.P.O.* in *Juristiche Wochenschrift*, 1927, p. 1297.

[6] *Jur. Wochenschrift*, 1927, p. 1297.

court may be made arbitrator and its decision may be treated as an award,[1] but in order to have this effect a clear provision in the agreement would be necessary.[2] A German court has no power to restrain a party from bringing or pursuing an action in a foreign court in breach of a submission under German law. Under German law the rules determining the validity of a submission as to form, content and capacity of the parties are considered substantive law, whereas the effects of a submission and the provisions of the *Z.P.O.* relating to them are law of procedure. So the position is very similar to that under English law. As to the enforcement of a foreign award in Germany, German law of procedure is exclusively applicable as *lex fori*,[3] but in regard to the proceedings in a foreign reference and the form of an award under foreign law the foreign rules apply as *lex fori*,[4] if their validity is attacked in a German action. So in an action on a Belgian award which based in its procedure partly on a judgment of a Belgian court in Antwerp the German court held that although this judgment would not be recognized as such in Germany because of want of reciprocity with Belgium (§ 328, *Z.P.O.*) the award based on it was nevertheless good, if good according to Belgian procedure law.[5]

A German court cannot set aside a foreign award because, besides other practical reasons, the foreign procedure law would then have to be applied, but a foreign award may not be enforced by a German court, as this is a question of German procedure.[6] In an action on a foreign award all the available defences under the foreign law may be pleaded, and therefore it seems that in an action on an English award in Germany the objections possible are wider [7] than they would be against a German award (see p. 21 *et seq.*).

Under German law there does not seem to be any objection to apply the remedies of enforcement provided by the Code also to foreign awards. And this is also the view of the *Reichsgericht* in several cases.[8] The decree for leave to enforce will be granted if the foreign award complies with

[1] *R.G.*, vol. 36, p. 383.

[2] Under English law these effects would result without express provision. See In the *Cap Blanco* [1913] P. 130.

[3] *R.G.*, vol. 5, p. 399.

[4] *R.G.*, vol. 30, p. 371.

[5] Decision of the R.G. of June 28, 1927, in *Jur. Wochenschrift*, 1927, p. 2312.

[6] Decision of the R.G. of February 22, 1927, in *Jur. Wochenschrift*, 1927, p. 1311. *R.G.*, vol. 116, p. 194, and decision of the R.G. of February 7, 1928, in *Jur. Wochenschrift* 1928, p. 1223.

[7] Decision of the *Oberlandesgericht*, Hamburg, of October 31, 1924; *Hanseatische Rechtszeitschrift*, 1925, p. 63, copied in Nussbaum's *Yearbook*, vol. i, p. 278.

[8] *R.G.*, vol. 5, p. 399; vol. 30, p. 368. Beschluss of Oberlandesgericht Köln of June 25, 1925, in *Jur. Wochenschrift* 1926, p. 1609.

The statement of Mr. Weiss in 43 *L.Q.R.*, p. 209, "On the whole the courts in Germany seem to be inclined to view awards obtained abroad with suspicion, and it happens, frequently enough, that notwithstanding the existence of the foreign award the party relying on it is compelled for some technical reason or other to start proceedings *de novo*," is without proper foundation.

the formal requirements of § 1039, *Z.P.O.* as *lex fori*. They are, as we have seen, on pp. 23, 28 above, an award must be dated and signed by all the arbitrators. A copy of the award, signed by the arbitrators, must be served on the parties and the original award is to be filed with the clerk of the proper court together with proof of such service.

It seems that only a German court can be the proper court for the above purpose (Beschluss of the Court in Cologne, see note 8, p. 35).

This practice of granting leave to enforce foreign awards was established before the statutory amendment of February 24, 1924 (*Imperial Law Gazette*, vol. i, p. 135 ss), but since then difficulties have arisen. Before the amendment the remedy of enforcing awards (German and foreign) as provided by the *Z.P.O.* was an execution judgment after a hearing of the application, and an application for such judgment could be opposed for the same reasons as would entitle a party to have an award set aside by action. But by the statutory amendment of § 1042, *Z.P.O.*, the court may in a simplified procedure either grant leave to enforce or stay the motion if the defendant proves that he has instituted proceedings to set aside the award within the time fixed by the court; but in both cases it cannot in this motion try questions of objections taken. Now in the case of foreign awards the proceedings to set aside an award can by German law only be taken in the proper foreign court. Therefore a German court would, since the Statutory Amendment, not be competent any longer to determine before its tribunal objections taken to a foreign award by way of defence as it was before. Therefore the conclusions have been drawn by Jonas [1] that foreign awards are not to be enforced by the simplified procedure of the *Z.P.O.* to grant leave to enforce, but only by action, as otherwise the position of the plaintiff would be unduly hard, as the stay on account of protracted proceedings in a foreign country court may cause great delay. The *Reichsgericht* considered the position arising under the new statutory amendment in a recent case, but left its own decision doubtful as it was not a point in issue.[2]

If the simplified procedure should be refused in future to foreign awards there remains always the ordinary action to enforce a foreign award, and the position would be very much like that under English law with its distinction between the procedure of leave to enforce and of setting aside an award. In an action on an award the defendant will be able to plead [3] by way of defence all irregularities available under the foreign law in question (by analogy to § 1041, s. 1, *Z.P.O.*). Intentional disregard of compulsory provisions of the German law could, however, not be pleaded. As to the other sections of § 1041, *Z.P.O.*, applicable

[1] *Jur. Wochenschrift*, 1927, p. 1299 ss.

[2] Decision of the R.G. in *R.G.*, vol. 116, p. 194, and of Febuary 7, 1928, in *Jur. Wochenschrift*, 1928, p. 1223; see also Prof. Kisch in *Jur. Wochenschrift*, 1927, p. 1376, and Leo in *J.W.*, 1928, p. 1453, who consider the position unsatisfactory, but seem to admit the new procedure of § 1042, Z.P.O., also for foreign awards.

[3] *Jur. Wochenschrift*, 1927, p. 1229 s.

by analogy, the German court would have to apply German law, but as to ss. 4 and 5 a submission under a foreign law, which does not make the same formal requirements as under these sections may constitute a waiver of irregularities under these sections.

Under German law submission and award follow contract principles [1] and therefore an award which is valid according to the law under which the parties compromised has its immediate effect like any other contract if brought before a German court. It may be that the special simplified procedure of enforcement is refused if the award does not comply with the German rules, but as a contract it has its effect nevertheless. It has this effect without a foreign court interfering, and its effect is even stronger where a foreign judgment would not be recognized by a German court because of want of reciprocity. An order by the foreign court granting leave to enforce an award governed by its laws, as *e.g.* leave to enforce an English award by a Master of the High Court under s. 12 of the Arbitration Act, would not be considered as a judgment of a foreign court by German law (see decision in note below), not because of its form,[2] but because according to the German conception the English courts are not competent to grant leave to enforce with effect as against Germany. And this is, I submit, also the correct view in accordance with the English law, because the Arbitration Act did not empower an English court to grant leave to enforce an award outside the jurisdiction or to do constitutive acts such as to direct judgment to be enforced in accordance with an award, if leave to enforce is sought. The only power conferred under s. 12 is that "judgment may issue on the award."[3] This important distinction under English law clearly confirms the above view.

The Case of Merrifield, Ziegler & Co. v. Liverpool Cotton Association, Ltd.—The decision of Eve J. in the case of *Merrifield, Ziegler & Co.* v. *Liverpool Cotton Association, Ltd.* [1911] L.T. 105, p. 97, has received great attention by English legal writers, and is usually cited as authority in English textbooks[4] for the proposition that an award made by foreign arbitrators (better, foreign awards), which is by the law of the foreign country not enforceable without an order of the courts of that country, is not a judgment of a foreign tribunal, which can be enforced by action in English courts. This proposition, I submit, is correct as far as it goes, but it cannot be used to support the following propositions: (1) that a foreign award cannot be sued on in England without an enforcement order of the foreign country; and (2) that a foreign award, to which

[1] Nussbaum in *Yearbook*, vol. i, p. 14, with legal literature quoted; *R.G.*, vol. 30, p. 370.

[2] *R.G.*, vol. 16, p. 428.

[3] *In re Willesden Local Board and Wright* [1896] 2 Q.B. 417; Russell, *op. cit.*, pp. 267–8.

[4] Russell, *op. cit.*, p. 274; Dicey, *Conflict of Laws*, 4th ed., p. 433; Bacon, *op. cit.*, pp. 114–15; but, more correct, Westlake, *Private International Law*, 7th ed., by Bentwich, § 331 a.

an enforcement order was granted by the foreign country, would be a foreign judgment, on which an action could be brought in England. The point in issue in the above case as far as it concerns us here was shortly stated as follows: An action was brought in the High Court to enforce a German award. The award was held to be binding and valid according to German law by the learned judge at the trial, but the action was dismissed, because the plaintiffs had not affirmatively proved that under German law a German submission imports an implied contract to perform the award, and failing this the German award could not be held to be a foreign judgment which the English court would recognize as such.

Whilst the ruling of the learned judge that a German award is not a foreign judgment is correct, the other considerations, I submit, cannot be followed for these reasons:

(1) Under English law an English submission imports, as we have seen, an implied promise to perform the award. This implied contract is one by implication of law, not by implication of fact,[1] and is nothing else than law in the ordinary sense, but not a contract. As Lord Mansfield puts it in an early case,[2] "If the defendant be under an obligation, from the test of natural justice, to refund, the law implies a debt and gives this action, founded in the equity of the plaintiff's case, as it were upon a contract (*quasi ex contractu*, as the Roman law expresses it)." Lindley L.J. says[3]: "Owing to the unfortunate terminology of our law . . . the expression "implied contract" has been used not only to denote a genuine contract established by inference, but also an obligation which does not arise from any real contract, but which can be enforced as if it had a contractual origin. Obligations of this class are called by the civilians obligations *quasi ex contractu*." I submit that this legal rule of an implied promise to perform an award is not, or at any rate not solely, an institute of the English substantive law, but one which is equally adjective law or law of procedure. In support of this view I quote Odgers on the Common Law, 3rd ed., vol. ii, p. 305: "The law, therefore, in order to give the plaintiff a *remedy*, assimilates to contracts certain cases in which there clearly is no contractual relation whatever between the parties. These we may best describe as "quasi-contracts," for that term in itself denotes that they are not contracts at all, but that the law will treat them as if they were. The *remedy* is analogous to, and in the form of, an action on a contract, because otherwise no remedy would exist." That the view taken above is correct becomes very clear when one considers the nature of a contract implied by English law to satisfy a foreign judgment.

[1] Thus an action may lie against a defendant for an implied contract for money had and received though he may have protested against such a contract. *Gore* v. *Gibson* [1845] 13 M. & W. 623–626. A different category are the contracts implied by implication of fact. They are real contracts.

[2] *Moses* v. *Macferlan* [1760] 2 Burrows, 1005, 1008.

[3] *In re Rhodes* v. *Rhodes* [1890] 44 Ch.D.P. 107.

If the quasi-contract were substantive law then inquiries would have to be made whether the foreign law also implies a quasi-contract. These inquiries cannot be made because they would be against the purpose of this rule of law. Therefore the right inference to be drawn is that in the case of a foreign judgment the implied quasi-contract is part of the law of remedies; and in the case of an implied contract to perform an award, the conclusion cannot be different for the above general reasons. The result is that an English court cannot in an action to enforce a foreign award inquire whether a foreign submission has, by the foreign law, the effect of giving rise to an action on the award, but the English court has to apply its own law of procedure. Any such inquiry is even more clearly excluded if by the foreign law the remedy of an action on the award is conceived to be law of procedure.[1] In my view there is in fact no quasi-contract imported into a German submission by German law. The German law did not build up any such construction; all that it did was to give a remedy to enforce a foreign award. The German *R.G.* says literally:[2] " If it is legal to refer disputes to foreign arbitration, there must be a way to give effect to the contractual intention of the parties, if there is an award valid according to the foreign law, although not complying with the provisions of the *Z.P.O.* This way is the present action, which seeks for the performance of an award made in accordance with the submission. The necessity for such a remedy has already been urged by the *Reichsoberlandesgericht.*" By a curious chance this decision was in a case on an English award, and the German *R.G.* rightly did not even put the question whether an English submission imported a quasi-contract to perform an award. We have already seen on p. 30 that the remedy by way of action is as a rule refused to German awards by reason of the principle of economy prevailing in the German law of procedure. But that would not justify the conclusion—if there were really quasi-contracts of the nature of substantive law in both countries—to refuse to a German award in England an action on an award, because the German procedure provides for its own awards a more economic and simplified method of enforcing.

In concluding, I submit respectfully that the decision in the *Merrifield, Ziegler*, etc., case labours under the defect that the English judge did not apply the English law of procedure, but made inquiries as to the foreign law of procedure.[3]

(2) But there is another consideration in the decision which requires comment. It seems that the court would have been prepared to treat

[1] *R.G.*, vol. 30, p. 371. [2] *Ibid.*

[3] Oppenheimer, in commenting on the decision in Nussbaum's *Yearbook*, vol. i, p. 289, does not touch the root of the problem, but cites a decision of the *R.G.*, which apparently relates to German law of procedure. In the subsequent comment, p. 295 s., on the case *In re Bankers and Shippers Insurance Co. of New York* v. *Liverpool Marine and General Insurance Co., Ltd.*, he does not show whether the American law imports a quasi-contract into the submission which would be against the conclusions drawn by him.

the award as a foreign judgment if an enforcement order could have been made in Germany. The enforcement order would have been in 1911 still in the form of an enforcement judgment, and all grounds for setting aside could have been pleaded by the defendant in the course of this litigation. But I submit that an enforcement judgment should not have been treated by the English court like a foreign judgment any more than to-day a simple decree for leave to enforce ought to be so regarded. The formula of a German enforcement judgment before 1924 was simply [1] "Execution may ensue out of this award . . .," and the same formula is still used to-day.[2] This is clearly not a foreign judgment *in rem* or *in personam*, which the English courts could recognize. It certainly does not condemn a party to pay a certain sum,[3] and it is not the judgment of a competent court, because only an English court can give leave to enforce an award or allow an action on an award with effect for England. Therefore I think the principle *Exequatur sur exequator ne vaut*[4] holds good for English law.

The proper conclusions, therefore, are that an English court cannot for the enforcement of a foreign award require an enforcement order of that country, and if such an enforcement order should have been given it is without value for proceedings in an English court. It cannot be denied that an enforcement order of a foreign country in respect of a foreign award may seem to save an English judge the very difficult task of examining a foreign award from the point of view of the foreign law; but what if the foreign enforcement order is only a clerical one without entering in the merits as in Belgium (Code de proc. civ., Art 1020) or a litigious one but not on the merits, as in Germany? In an action on a German award before an English court the court may have to consider only in one instance and incidentally whether a German enforcement order was made, because according to German law, § 1044, the right of the defendant to bring an action to set aside an award may be extinguished by lapse of time, and he would therefore be unable to raise objections before an English court after the lapse of that time.

The only possible way[5] to treat awards is according to the principles applying to contracts, and any other principle would destroy the great scope which arbitration offers for giving effect to foreign awards where judgments for reasons of sovereignty and also the doctrine of reciprocity could not be effectual in the foreign country.

From this aspect the decision in the case of *Merrifield, Ziegler*, etc., is a great danger, as is shown by the conclusions drawn from it by English legal writers.

[1] Sydow-Busch, *Z.P.O.*, 16th ed., p. 918. [2] Stein, *op. cit.*, vol. ii, p. 1067.
[3] Dicey, p. 433 ss.; Westlake, p. 394 ss. [4] Nussbaum, *Yearbook*, vol. i, p. 31.
[5] *Ibid.*, p. 14. The doctrine of contract is prevalent, in Belgium, France, Germany and Holland.

FSC
www.fsc.org
MIX
Papier | Fördert gute Waldnutzung
FSC® C083411

Kolibri 360 GmbH
Ferdinand-Jühlke-Straße 7
99095 Erfurt, Deutschland
produktsicherheit@kolibri360.de